Rwanda
RISING FROM THE ASHES

An inspiring account of the
ministry of a white Rwandan Bishop:
The Right Revd Kenneth Barham OBE

John Miles

First published 2011

ISBN No: 978-1-907636-33-2

Published by Verité CM Ltd for John Miles
Cover design, typesetting and production management
by Verité CM Ltd, Worthing, West Sussex UK
+44 (0) 1903 241975

Printed in Denmark
by Nørhaven, Viborg

Contents

by Lord Carey of Clifton.
Former Archbishop of Canterbury, 1991-2002

In April 1994, a horrified world learned that in the beautiful, land-locked country of Rwanda – a country where Christianity was, and is, the dominant religion – a genocide had taken place which cost the lives of over a million people. My wife and I paid an official visit to the country a few months after the genocide and were shocked by the situation that greeted us- divided and guilty churches and communities; vengeful and grieving families; distrustful and watchful politicians and community leaders.

Questions are still being asked about this terrible event. What caused it? What were the political reasons? Why were so many faith leaders caught up in the madness and failed to give a true Christian response? How is it possible that, in a country where Christianity was so vibrant, this faith failed to stop the massacre of thousands of people?

One way of tracing the roots of the genocide is through the eyes of someone whose love, knowledge and experience of Rwanda goes back to his early years. For me, and so many Christians in England, Rwanda is synonymous with the Barham family. Lawrence, Ken's father, served as a missionary teacher in Rwanda for many years. Lawrence was central to the East Africa Revival which swept through the region, touching the lives of thousands. Through the labours of missionaries like Joe Church and Lawrence Barham and many others, the church became indigenous and confident.

Hence the burning question: Why?

The answers come indirectly through this book and through the biography of Bishop Kenneth Barham.

Ken is one of the most unassuming Christian leaders I know but we should not let that fool us. He is one of the most courageous, determined and focused people I know. The story reveals his development as a Christian, his call, his marriage to Jill (whose story alongside Ken's is no less appealing and sacrificial) and their joint ministry both in the UK and in Rwanda. The genocide of 1994 plunged them both into a nightmare world in which familiar signposts were torn out and thrown away. Ken's leadership was tested in many different ways and this book reveals the challenges he and Jill faced as they tried, with others, to restore faith, fan the weak flames of hope and begin again.

The question 'Why?' is still one that has not been answered properly.

What this book reveals are depths of political complicity that are deeply shocking. Ken and other leaders knew that the outside world was already aware of the deep unrest in the region. Even though United Nations troops were in the country at the time, little effort was made by the international community to intervene. The French government still has questions to answer for its role in the breakdown of Rwanda. It is a shameful and shocking story of neglect by Western powers.

The great thing about Bishop Ken is that he still wants to carry on investing in Rwanda. The Christian faith is not keen on deaths; It is a resurrection faith and that is the philosophy that Ken shares. Although retired, he and Jill continue to uphold the church in Rwanda in their prayers and in their giving. This is an inspiring story but, then, again, the Barhams are an inspiring family. This is a book for our times.

While on a visit to our daughter in Costa Rica my brief case was stolen containing my blood pressure tablets. The local doctor tried to match them, but the pressure went up too high and I was told to take a complete rest. The family suggested I wrote some of my adventures in Africa. While taking groups to Rwanda over the years many people said "you must write your story". In 2010 Paul Settatree, who went to Rwanda as a VSO in 1967, urged a friend of his, John Miles, to persuade me to allow him to write my story. John has worked in missions in many nations of the world and until recently was Director for Africa for the missions organisation International Teams. He has a Masters Degree in Missions from the Birmingham Bible Institute. His books are *'Overcoming the power of hell'* about the LRA in Uganda, *'Are we nearly there yet?'* and *'To catch a thief'*. John said "if you can find a publisher I will write a book".

We had been given some free tickets for the Christian Resources Exhibition, so we went. We visited all the stalls which mentioned publishing. Most of them were pretty negative. We got to a stall marked *Verité Christian Resources*. We talked to Chris Powell at the stall who, after so many negative replies, to our surprise said very positively "Yes I will happily publish a book for you". We are grateful to Chris and John and we pray that some of the accounts of God's protection and the amazing way in which the Lord sent the funds for our projects will be an encouragement to others to trust in God. We are also grateful to Archbishop George Carey for sparing the time to write the Foreword.

We found it quite amusing to see how the same

event had quite different memories for us. Our daughter Sue remembers my Consecration in Cyangugu in 1993. She says "I remember being in the house trying to make Grandpa's robes fit you better – and the funny hat! I remember making those flags with the Anglican Church symbol to try and ease your way through the road blocks. I remember all sitting on the edge of the bath looking for jiggers, and going to the market with Jane to look for pretty fabric. I remember little of the details of the service, just the setting in the stadium, and what I would consider a typical 'African' service/celebration, lots of colours, lots of singing and the choirs, but nothing of what was said – sorry. Oh, and then there was your pet crane who didn't like me at all, and kept going after me in the kitchen – which I didn't like because I consider myself good with animals!"

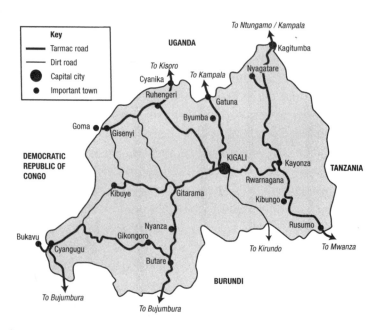

CHAPTER ONE

Evil Descending

The sudden outbreak of mass murder, violence and rape that descended on Rwanda in April 1994 traumatised the nation and shocked a world that looked on in horror, but seemed powerless to stop. In approximately one hundred days, an estimated one million people, overwhelmingly of the Tutsi ethnic group, were slaughtered; mostly with clubs and machetes. Subsequent investigations of these events by international organisations such as the United Nations, led to them being officially classified as 'Genocide'. Extreme elements of the majority Hutu ethnic group embarked on a campaign of unspeakable violence aimed at their Tutsi neighbours and anyone who tried to defend them. Bewildered Tutsis suddenly found that some of their long-standing neighbours who had lived ordinary lives, in some cases even attended the same churches, were now their mortal enemies. Tutsis who fled to Hutu friends for refuge often found that they were turned away for fear that they themselves would also be targeted by the extremists if they aided any Tutsis, or even spoke out against the violence.

Up to half a million women were brutally raped and many killed – all were Tutsis. Rape was systematic and used as a weapon. It was perpetrated with sickening violence. The rapes have led to an escalation in Rwanda of the AIDS pandemic that blights most of Africa. Some fled to churches only to die in the flames and fumes as the church building was set alight by the killers. Other Tutsis tried to hide in churches hoping for sanctuary, but the churches were searched and any Tutsis or sympathisers found there were murdered or raped, or both.

For the Right Reverend Kenneth Barham, Bishop of Cyangugu, (an Anglican Diocese in southern Rwanda), and concurrently Vicar of Ashburnham & Penhurst Parishes in Sussex, England – Ken to his friends – what he thought was going to be an ordinary day in his parish work at home in the UK, turned into horror. It was April 7th 1994 when Ken and his wife Jill switched on the television news as usual at 10.00 pm, only to hear that ethnic violence had broken out in his beloved Rwanda. This beautiful land of mountains and forests, where he had lived with his missionary parents from the age of two until he came to England at the age of nineteen, was in turmoil. Rwanda and Kenya had largely formed him, educated him and was deeply embedded into his very being. It is impossible to overstate the impact that this news had on him.

For Ken Barham, this was not just another of the world's disasters being sensationalised by the media; this hit him personally. In the days and weeks that followed, normal patterns of life ceased in the Barham household. All the news broadcasts on the television riveted his attention and dominated his day. Over the next week he recorded every main news broadcast, morning and evening. Many short snippets of news which meant little or nothing to most people were vital clues to Ken and Jill in hearing what was happening in Rwanda. The snippets had to be reviewed and inserted into the jigsaw of horror and disbelief that was rapidly forming in their minds and tormenting their souls. To this day he retains this large collection of VCR tapes. He craved news; especially about his own Diocese of Cyangugu (pronounced Chun-googoo), but it wasn't mentioned. Was no news, good news? Countless times he tried to phone friends and church colleagues, but the telephone lines were down throughout Rwanda and he endured the agony of not knowing the situation there. Had the killing reached Cyangugu, in this relatively remote part of Rwanda? Had the Tutsis among his friends been able to escape? A kaleidoscope of nightmarish thoughts tormented his mind and hope was hard to grasp. Ken later learned that all but one of the Rwandan House of Bishops had fled the country, regardless of whether they were Tutsi or Hutu; no one was safe. In fact, at that time, only one was a Tutsi. Even if the phone lines had still been working, some of those he most needed to speak to had gone.

Ken had been visiting Rwanda as part of his work with the Ruanda Mission and later as a Canon of Butare Cathedral, raising funds in UK and channelling them through the Lawrence Barham Memorial Trust (a charity registered in the UK, which Ken named after his father) twice a year for the previous twelve years.

He had recently returned in February from the latest of his regular trips. He would have been catching up with his normal parish work, but this event brought things to a sudden halt. Every time Ken returned home from Rwanda to his family and quiet English parishes, he left part of his soul behind in the land that he loved so much. Now the worst thing that could possibly happen in Rwanda was unfolding before Ken and Jill as they sat transfixed by the news reports. Every day it seemed that the situation became worse. Ken's overriding thought was that he must get back to Rwanda. He had to see what was happening to his many friends and colleagues in Cyangugu. Without normal communications he had no way of knowing. It was agonising.

What later became clear to Ken and to those who had the responsibility of investigating the Genocide, was that this was not spontaneous – it had been carefully planned. It was planned at the highest level in the military and even the Cabinet of President Juvenal Habyarimana's government, and executed with a brutal efficiency that surpassed anything perpetrated by the Nazis in their Second World War death camps in its cruelty, speed and intensity.

What possessed people, who were one day friends and neighbours, to suddenly turn into vile killers and rapists? It seems utterly incredible. Apparently ordinary people who loved their children and wives, who had been kind and helpful to their neighbours, who went regularly to church – some were even church officers – had suddenly turned into evil killing machines. If one speaks to Africans or those who know Africa well about this period, they might tell you that 'possessed' is an appropriate adjective to use. Given an open door into men's souls, there are a multitude of evil demonic forces ready to take control of men's minds and actions, fuelled by alcohol and drugs. Then, any evil is possible and all hell breaks loose, as history from many parts of the world will testify. In April 1994 many in Rwanda opened that door, and the results were horrendous. In the early days and weeks of the violence, the outside world had little idea of the disaster that was unfolding in the beautiful land of Rwanda. Mass killings are officially designated as 'Genocide' when they are carried out by a government or government sponsored groups and target a particular ethnic group, tribe or religion. The horror that spread throughout Rwanda in April 1994 was Genocide in every aspect of that chilling concept.

*　　*　　*

CHAPTER TWO

A Good Inheritance

When people talk about inheritance, they are usually referring to money or property. However, there is a far more important inheritance, a spiritual inheritance – which can be good or bad. Ken Barham was privileged to have an exceptionally good one.

Ken's early years in his missionary home in Africa were idyllic. His parents, Lawrence and Julia were part of a team of missionaries, in which they were among the foremost leaders in the spiritual awakening that has become known as 'The Rwanda revival'.

The Belgian authorities – influenced partly by the Catholic Church – had been resisting any influx of Protestant missionaries. While they waited for the opportunity to expand the work into Rwanda, they worked in Kabale which was under British rule. Their second child, Ken was born there on 1st March 1936 in the midst of a revival.

Ken's mother, Julia, had grown up in colonial Kenya. Her father, Canon Leakey, (left) arrived in Kabete, Kenya in 1899 and spent many years translating the Bible into the Kikuyu language, which was spoken by millions of Kenyans of that tribe; the largest in Kenya.

One of Julia's brothers, Dr Louis Leakey, was well known as an anthropologist. He and his wife Mary spent many years digging for prehistoric human remains at Olduvai Gorge, Lake Rudolph and other places. His mother's sister, Gladys was married to the Archbishop of East Africa, Dr Leonard Beecher (both pictured above), who was also Ken's godfather. Julia's younger brother, Douglas, was head of the Forestry at Nyeri, near Mount Kenya.

Louis and Mary Leakey

Ken's mother was good at languages and was fluent in Kikuyu. She had grown up among the Kikuyu and went on to found a girls' secondary school at Kabete, outside Nairobi, which is still one of the leading schools in Kenya – the Mary Leakey Secondary School. Ken lived with the

Leakeys and the Beechers at Limuru, Kenya, for two years during the war. Louis and Mary were very kind to him when he was a pupil at the Duke of York School. They lived not far away, at the edge of the Nairobi Game Park, and used to take him out at weekends. Their three children, Jonathan, Richard and Philip are third generation Kenyans and are all involved in Kenyan life. When Mary died the family asked Ken to take a memorial service for her *'because Ken was the only religious member of the family!'* When back in England, he made some enquiries and found that Jesus College, Cambridge was where she had gained one of her doctorates, so he arranged a memorial service in the college chapel.

Ken's father, Lawrence, was born in 1901 and grew up in Wimbledon. He won a scholarship to Merchant Taylor's School and another to Gonville and Caius College, Cambridge, where he read classics. He had a brilliant mind. He achieved a First Class Degree in Hebrew, winning the Stewart of Rannoch and Tyrwhitt Hebrew Scholarships and the Mason Hebrew prize. He was offered a post as a university Don, specialising in Hebrew and Aramaic. He turned down this attractive offer of a fine academic career because he believed that God had a higher calling for him – to missionary work. He served his curacy at St James, Hatcham where he met and became friends with a student at Goldsmiths College, Julia Leakey, Ken's mother. If there was an immediate attraction between them, they knew it was pointless because she was preparing to return to teaching in Kenya and he was preparing to go to China with the Church Missionary Society (CMS).

One of the things often misunderstood about missionaries and their children, is the place they consider as their 'home'. Julia Leakey had been raised in Kenya. She was in fact a 'white Kenyan'. For her, visiting England was visiting a foreign country. Returning to Kenya was 'going home'. She was going home to all the places, languages, culture and familiar surrounding that she had known and loved from her earliest days.

For Lawrence, the opposite was true. He had grown up in post World War One London. However, his plans were to change! In 1927 the political situation in China was uncertain because the civil war, that eventually brought the Communists to power, had begun. This uncertainty had caused the Council of CMS to stop Lawrence going to China and asked him to go to Uganda instead. So, in 1928, Lawrence sailed for Kenya. He took the train from Mombasa to Nairobi, where the Secretary of the Society in Kenya, Canon Harry Leakey met him. He took him to their house in Kabete and to his surprise and delight there was Julia, back from London. It was a divine appointment!

They were married a few years later in 1931, and worked at Kabale in south-west Uganda with the Ruanda Mission of the CMS. Lawrence started as Headmaster of Kigezi High School. He spent many days walking in the rural areas in Bufumbira, setting up churches. He soon mastered the local language, Lukiga, and started a Bible teaching ministry. In 1934 he built a Bible College which has since developed into the Bishop Barham University College, Kabale, a constituent college of the Uganda Christian University, Kampala, Uganda's capital city.

Ken's elder sister, Barbara, was born that year. On 1st March 1936 Ken was born in the house of Dr Joe Church, and brought into the world by his godfather, Dr Jack Symonds. These doctors and others worked at Kabale while waiting for permission from the Belgian government to go into Ruanda-Urundi. Permission was only given when British engineers were preparing to build a railway from Cape to Cairo. They asked the Belgians for Church of England clergy to take services for them. The railway never materialised, but the way into Belgian administered Ruanda-Urundi was opened! In 1938, ten years after Lawrence had arrived in Africa, Urundi (modern day Burundi) opened up and the Barham family moved to a new home at Ibuye.

Ken's parents were able to join the first missionary movement with the Ruanda Mission into what was called then Ruanda-Urundi. The mission realised that they needed a geographically central training school for church teachers and clergy ordinands. They were posted to Ibuye in Burundi where they began building the centre and teaching the new converts. Although the Belgian authorities allowed the mission to set up mission stations, they were restricted to doing this in rural areas. They didn't want the Protestant missions in town centres where the Catholic churches were situated.

The Mission set up three centres in Ruanda and three in Urundi. Ibuye was one of the centres and Ken's parents built a church, a school and a college and others built the hospital. This building programme of church, school and hospital took place in all the centres established by the Ruanda Mission. The aim was to begin to meet the needs of the local people for the Christian faith, education and medical provision. The centres had to be built on land granted by the Belgian authorities and approved by the local chief. The finances for this came from committed individuals back home who saw the importance of this work. The ministry of the missionaries was mightily blessed by God and the number of converts began to multiply as the Revival that began at Gahini in Ruanda spread to Kabale in Uganda and throughout Ruanda-Urundi.

The church that Ken's parents built was large enough to be the cathedral and they went on to build a theological seminary with about a dozen small houses for the married students with families. This is now called the 'College Theologique Bishop Barham'. Ken's mother Julia was given the task of teaching the wives.

Buye Cathedral

Lawrence Barham didn't believe in getting into debt. As money was sent by praying people back home, he did the work. When money ran out he stopped until more money came in and the building could recommence. The nearby river bed provided ideal clay for making bricks which were then fired in a brick kiln in the traditional African way. When this substantial building was complete in 1940, the stop-start phases of building can be seen in the slightly differing brick colours.

In 1946, Lawrence was nominated to be Bishop of Ruanda-Urundi. The Bishop of Uganda rejected this because of Lawrence's deep involvement with the East African Revival. At that time, the revival was viewed with some apprehension by the Church of Uganda leadership. In 1957, Lawrence returned to Uganda for two years as Archdeacon of Ankole-Kigezi. In 1958, Lawrence and Julia retired from active missionary service in Africa to take on the duties of General Secretary of the Ruanda Mission (CMS). On the retirement of the first Bishop of Rwanda and Burundi in 1964, Lawrence was consecrated as his successor in Namirembe Cathedral. For the next two years he concentrated on the preparation of African bishops for the newly formed separate dioceses of Rwanda and Burundi. In 1966, he and Julia retired to the U.K. and were active in their retirement to the last.

Bishop Lawrence Barham with his assistant
Bishop Yohana Nkunzumwami

On his retirement he was offered a post at Emmanuel Church Wimbledon, which he accepted. When he was licensed, Bishop Mervyn Stockwood asked if he would also be an Assistant Bishop of Southwark Diocese. He agreed provided he could wear only convocation robes of Chimere, Rochet and Black Scarf. The Bishop agreed and wrote to all his clergy saying that Bishop Barham would only use those robes when officiating in any of the churches. Lawrence died aged seventy two in 1973 having served his God faithfully and with humility all his life, achieving more than most.

The place names all changed with Independence in 1962, Rwanda and Burundi were separated and the country names were changed. Ibuye became Buye and is now the cathedral centre of one of the dioceses of Burundi.

At the age of five Ken went to a boarding school for missionaries' children, Kabale Prep School. His memories of that school are all happy ones. He cannot remember anyone being unhappy at KPS! From there he went to boarding schools at the age of nine, in Eldoret and Nairobi. There were no mixed race schools in colonial Nairobi at that time. There was the Duke of York, the Prince Wales School for boys and the Kenya High School for girls. Kenya high School was known to the boys of Prince of Wales School as 'the heifer boma' – the compound for the young cows! There was also a girls' school at Limuru and an American school, the Rift Valley Academy, at Kijabe. These were all for white people. In our present time, this would be regarded as some kind of apartheid, but in those colonial days it was considered as normal and the children there knew no other life. Gradually other secondary schools were established, one for Asians and the Alliance High School for Africans.

Ken enrolled at The Duke of York School in 1950. All these boarding schools were fee paying and Ken's parents had to find the fees for all five of their children. On their missionary allowances this was humanly impossible. Ken learned an important lesson from them about faith. He clearly remembers them saying, before they started the journey to school for the start of any term, 'If the fees don't come soon, you won't be going.'

The postal system in Burundi was very poor. Letters had to be brought from Kabale in Uganda, which had a postal service, carried on someone's head, because there was no public transport. When the weary travellers reached Kampala there was usually post waiting to be collected. More than once, there in the CMS post box was a letter to Ken's parents with money that covered their school fees. In later life, these important lessons in faith would serve him well as he sought to raise large amounts of money for the work in Cyangugu.

Ken's first visit to England was in 1939 as a baby. The next was in 1946 when, as a ten year old, his parents came home for their furlough. They had come by ship from Mombasa, through the Red Sea and the Suez Canal. The ship was the 'SS Alcantara'. Also on board was a large consignment of Italian prisoners of war from Kenya. The vessel called at Naples where the prisoners disembarked, giving a lot more room in the ship. For Ken it was a great adventure of discovery as they sailed on through the Bay of Biscay and up the English Channel to Southampton. The journey took three weeks, with numerous stops and he saw some fascinating places. Ken arrived in England, which was to him a strange country; a place that throughout his young life people had referred to as 'Home'.

Ken spent a year at St. Michael's School, Limpsfield, Surrey to give him some continuity in his education. While there, in 1947, Ken caught measles with the added complication of Encephalitis. His sister Bar saw him being carried out of the san on a stretcher foaming at the mouth. His mother was with him in the Redhill County Hospital. She got a message to his father saying he was dying and he should come immediately. His father was one of the speakers at a conference in Hildenborough Hall with Dr Joe Church, who said "before you go we must pray". By the time Lawrence arrived at the hospital, the doctor said "amazingly, he has turned the corner". It took weeks of Penicillin injections and supported walking before he was back to full strength, but God had worked a miracle that day in the life of an eleven year old schoolboy. The memories of the visit are still embedded in his mind. They arrived during one of the most severe winters ever recorded in Britain. All the pipes froze in the house which the family had been loaned, which was Rock House, The Ridge, Woldingham. It is an address Ken remembers clearly even though it was more than sixty years ago. It was his introduction to life in England and a shocking contrast to the relatively benign climate of East Africa. Although it was bitterly cold, young Ken, with Bar, Peter, Ian and Sheila, found the deep snow was great fun! In complete contrast, the following summer was unusually hot and reminded the family of Africa. They spent a week at the CSSM children's beach mission at Frinton-on-Sea.

The return journey to Mombasa was in 1948 on the 'SS Llangybi Castle', where fortunately there were no Italian soldiers! Ken was isolated for some days with chicken pox, but recovered in time to take part in the fancy dress party. Ken and his brother Peter both won prizes as pirates and Ken won his first camera, a Brownie box camera.

The next trip to England followed in 1955 when the family came by air for the first time. The plane was a twin-engine prop Viking and they had to land for fuel at Wadi

Halfa, by the river Nile on the Sudan-Egypt border. They then had their first experience of sleeping in a hotel in Malta (at the airline's expense!) before flying on to Heathrow. The journey now took two days instead of three weeks. These days Ken flies over all these countries in eight hours, a journey he has done dozens of times since.

With this family history, perhaps it was almost inevitable that God would lead Ken back to Rwanda to make his own unique and important contribution to the family's African odyssey. It was families such as these, who – long after the soldiers had returned home or to their barracks – formed the backbone of the British Empire. In an age when European powers were carving up large parts of the world for their own benefit, there were also brave souls who ignored the dangers and went forth in Christ's name to take the Gospel, education and progress to less developed countries. Some pioneer missionaries even packed part of their luggage in coffins intended for their own burial. They had no intention of coming home while their task was yet unfinished. In some parts of Africa, only one missionary in ten lived to tell their stories to their grandchildren.

As a boy, Ken had total freedom to play in and around the mission station where his ear soon began to tune in to the local languages as well as his parents English. He watched with fascination as buildings around his home were constructed. In a child's way he joined in the excitement of it all. From an early age he gained the instinct to see things grow and develop. In many ways he later became 'A chip off the old block' following his father's example.

Around the mission station, at prep school, boarding school in Nairobi and later farming in Uganda, he acquired a working knowledge of local languages. These included

Kinyarwanda and Kirundi both local to his parents' mission station; later Luganga, the language of Buganda, the region of Uganda where he farmed. While at boarding school in Nairobi he learned Swahili, the lingua franca of East Africa. All these proved to be extremely useful in his future mission work. This then, was Ken Barham's inheritance, and when the time and the call came in a different age, he didn't hesitate to take up the challenge – it was in his blood!

With thanks I rejoice
In thy fatherly choice
Of my state and condition below;
If of parents I came
Who honoured thy name,
'Twas thy wisdom appointed it so.

Charles Wesley

CHAPTER THREE

Genocide Planned

For nothing is hidden that will not be revealed,
nor anything secret that will not be known
and come to light.
Luke 8:17

The brutal murder of a million people in just one hundred days, mainly with primitive weapons such as machetes and clubs, does not happen spontaneously. It has to be planned. In Rwanda in 1994, it had indeed been planned. Killing on such a scale with these simple weapons, requires a large number of perpetrators. It has been estimated that more than 200,000 Hutus took part in the killing. People do not wake up one morning and suddenly realise that they hate their neighbours. Hate them to the extent that they are prepared to systematically kill, rape and torture them without mercy. The minds of such killers have first to be conditioned, poisoned and prepared, in order for them to act in this inhuman way. Prior to the genocide of 1994 in Rwanda, this pre-conditioning of the minds of millions of citizens had taken place. We might compare the Rwandan Genocide with other atrocities such as the Nazi extermination camps for Jews, or 'ethnic cleansing' in the Balkans. They all have one thing in common; there is a long history to the conflict and ethnic hatred has been stirred up over many years.

Prior to the twentieth century, the Hutus and the Tutsis had managed to live in relative harmony with each other for hundreds of years, in the lands we now know as Rwanda and Burundi. It is as if, long ago, the Tutsi and Hutu had struck a deal with each other over the use of their beautiful land of mountains and forests. The Hutu farmed the land and the Tutsi kept cattle. They traded with each other and sometimes intermarried. Over hundreds of years, their language and culture became the same.

What went wrong? Where was the *'Most-High God'* to whom they all prayed in some form or other in their many churches or even in pagan rituals? Where was the Grace of the God and Father of the Lord Jesus Christ which had so famously been poured out on their land in revival-power not long ago? Such questions demand to be asked and demand, if at all possible, to be answered. What change took place in the largely harmonious relationship between these two ethnic groups with so much in common?

To find a point in history when things began to change, we cannot escape pointing the accusing finger at the intervention of the colonial powers. First the Germans, followed by the Belgians. The Germans' belief in the superiority of certain ethnic groups over others was, in their view, supported by what they observed in Rwanda. They came to believe that their Arian race was the master race. In the Tutsis they thought they had identified an ethnic group that had some descended similarities to their own, or at least European or Arab characteristics. They thought that they detected in them a superior race.

Belgium began to withdraw from Rwanda in 1959. In 1961 a Hutu-dominated government was established and Rwanda achieved Independence in 1962, replacing the colonial government of Belgium, which had ruled through the Tutsi royal family. One of the consequences of the Hutus gaining power was sporadic attacks on Tutsis and institutionalised repression that led to over 300,000 Tutsis fleeing, mainly to neighbouring countries over the next few years. For many Tutsi families it was the need for education for their children that became a major factor in the decision to flee.

Anti-Hutu attacks in neighbouring Burundi by the Tutsi-led government led to reprisal attacks against Tutsis in Rwanda in 1973. This resulted in even more refugees, many seeking asylum in Uganda. The land formerly owned by these thousands of refugees was subsequently claimed by others, creating another politically charged issue. By the 1980s, the Rwandan government of Juvénal Habyarimana claimed that the refugees could not return because there was no room in the country, which was already the most densely populated on the African continent. The Habyarimana regime also introduced further restrictions on Tutsis such as not being allowed to head any institution.

Throughout the 1970s and 1980s, Rwandan exiles formed political and military alliances, particularly in Uganda. The leader of one of these was Major General Fred Rwigema, Deputy Commander of the National Resistance Army (NRA). This was a Ugandan rebel group led by Yoweri Museveni, seeking to overthrow the brutal regime of Milton Obote in his second spell as President of Uganda, after he had ousted Idi Amin with the help of Tanzania. Fred Rwigema was a friend of Paul Kagame, whose family had fled to Uganda during the violence of 1959. In 1985, Kagame helped Fred Rwigema and others form the Rwandan Patriotic Front (RPF), an armed group aligned with the NRA. The RPF help, with their disciplined and well organised troops, was crucial to Museveni's victory and he determined that if and when the time came, he would return the favour.

It was a difficult time for Tutsi either in Rwanda or as refugees in Uganda. Education was often the most difficult issue. In Uganda they were discriminated against as refugees. In Rwanda they were seen as a people to be hated. One survivor recalls, 'All Tutsi children were made to stand up daily in class and the whole school was encouraged to despise them.' This survivor remembers coming home and asking her parents if she could stop being a Tutsi!

Paul Kagame became the head of NRA military intelligence and a close ally of Museveni. In 1986, the NRA rebellion succeeded and Museveni became President of Uganda. Then, as both a reward to an ally and in the hope that the large Rwandan refugee population in Uganda would return home, Museveni supported the RPF's unsuccessful invasion of Rwanda which began on 1st October 1990 and was led by Fred Rwigema. At the very start of the invasion Rwigema was killed and the RPF was routed. News reached Paul Kagame, who at the time was studying at a military training course at Fort Leavenworth, USA. He cut short his course and returned to Uganda, where he organised the regrouping of the RPF militia. Then, with an army of about 5,000 men and women, pitted against the French trained Rwandan army (FAR) which numbered 40,000, he invaded Rwanda again. The invasion resulted in a three year war and the occupation of much of the northern Rwandan districts of Byumba, Umutara and Ruhengeri. The invasion displaced many Hutus to other parts of the country and further heightened ethnic tensions.

The Arusha Accords

The 1993 Arusha Accords attempted to offer a diplomatic solution to both the RPF threat and the internal tensions, but it was never implemented. Ethnic tensions became even greater following the murder of Burundian President Melchior Ndadaye, a Hutu, in October 1993 – an event that sparked the Burundian Civil War in which large numbers of both Hutus and Tutsis were killed. Hutu militants, known as *Interahamwe* (which means those who work together), and senior elements in the Rwandan government began to plan the Genocide, with no lesser aim than to completely rid the country of their historical neighbours, the Tutsis.

Planning for the Genocide began earlier than 1993. In October 1992, Leon Mugesera, a member of the Hutu dominated MRND party which had close ties to the military, made a broadcast saying the Tutsi were not really Rwandans but Ethiopians. He stated that the Hutus didn't need to drive them out of Rwanda, because if they threw them in the river Nyabarongo they would float down to the Nile and thence back to Ethiopia from where he alleged they originated! His rhetoric escalated in an additional speech to about a thousand supporters on November 22nd where he said 'We the people are obliged to take responsibility ourselves and wipe out this scum!' He ranted that they should kill Tutsis and 'dump their bodies into the rivers of Rwanda.' In some of the photos of the Genocide there are many that show bodies floating in the river and choking up Lake Victoria.

Ironically, the national President of the Interahamwe militia, Robert Kajuga was from a Tutsi family whose father had acquired Hutu identity papers for his family. In order to avoid any kind of suspicion about their family being Tutsi, he kept his brother hidden at the Hotel des Mille Collins in Kigali.

The Arusha Accords were a set of five accords (or protocols) agreed in Arusha, Tanzania on August 4, 1993, by the government of Rwanda and the rebel Rwandan Patriotic Front, under mediation, to end the three-year long Rwandan Civil War. The five Accords established a broad-based transitional government that included the insurgent Rwandan

Patriotic Front (primarily Tutsi) with the five political parties that had composed a temporary government since April 1992 in anticipation of general elections.

It is important to note that because of the political impasse and preparations by extremists towards the Genocide that would occur in April 1994, the Arusha Accord never succeeded in creating a transitional government. Although each group was to be given different cabinet portfolios, it never materialized. Habyarimana constantly stalled the negotiations. The Rwandan Patriotic Front was granted participation in the national assembly. The Accords also provided the establishment of a military composed of sixty percent government troops and forty percent from the RPF. It was agreed that the transitional government and national assembly would be established no later than thirty-seven days after the signing of the Accords. The transitional period was limited to twenty-two months, after which general elections would be held. The delegations signed the protocol on August 3rd 1993, and President Habyarimana and RPF president Alexis Kanyarengwe signed the following day.

Intended as a negotiation for a sharing of power between the rebels and the Rwandan government, the talks produced an agreement that, in the eyes of Hutu extremists, favoured the Rwandan Patriotic Front. They believed that this was because of weakness and divisions within their own government. The opposition Foreign Minister, Boniface Ngulinzira, rather than Rwandan President Juvenal Habyarimana, led the government delegation and Habyarimana repeatedly vetoed the delegation's decisions. The Arusha Accords stripped many powers from the office of the President, transferring them to the transitional government. Some observers stated that President Habyarimana never intended to abide by the outcome of the talks. In November 1992, only midway through the talks, Habyarimana dismissively referred to the Arusha Accords as 'pieces of paper'. Hutu racial extremists aligned with President Habyarimana continued to be strongly opposed to sharing power with the former insurgency, and to the Accords, which called for them to lose control of the army and the government.

On October 5, 1993, the United Nations Security Council commissioned Resolution 872 which established the United Nations Assistance Mission for Rwanda (UNAMIR). Its objective was assistance in, and supervision of implementation of, the Arusha Accords. The initial U.N. presence was only 2,548 military personnel, largely Belgian soldiers. Once the killing began, they were totally ineffective.

Thus the scene was set. There was a pretence at finding a negotiated settlement, while at the same time Hutu extremist politicians were ordering thousands of machetes from China because they were cheap and available in large quantities. Without doubt, Genocide was their intention and they were secretly planning for this from an early stage.

In January 1994 Ken Barham made one of his regular month-long trips to Rwanda, this time in his newly consecrated role as assistant Bishop of Cyangugu. From this time, his main ministry was to be assisting Bishop Daniel Nduhura in building up the new diocese of Cyangugu. The country was in a heightened state of tension because of the RPF invasion and the Arusha talks in Tanzania. Much of the country was in limbo, not having an effective government. Lawlessness was on the increase as the country awaited the results of the talks. Ken didn't allow the situation to prevent him from making plans and advancing the work in Cyangugu. In the providence of God, he was not caught up in the violence that descended on Rwanda on 6th April.

He learned about it at home from the television news, and was available to return to help with the recovery in Cyangugu once it was over.

CHAPTER FOUR

The Land and Its People

The small Republic of Rwanda in East Central Africa is stunningly beautiful. It has often been called 'The Land of a Thousand Hills' or the 'Switzerland of Africa'. Its 26,300 square Kilometres (a similar size to Haiti or Wales) are intensively cultivated. With just under ten million people it is one of the most densely populated countries in the world.

Most people would have heard little about this country until the work of the American Zoologist Dian Fossey, sent there by Ken's uncle Dr Louis Leakey, over a period of eighteen years of studying and documenting the mountain gorillas in the remote Virunga Mountains. Her achievements became known through the popular Warner Bros. Film

'Gorillas in the Mist' (1988). The publicity was greatly appreciated by the Rwandan government because of the tourism it generated. This mountainous area is carefully preserved and one of the few places on earth where these wonderful animals are found in the wild. Sadly Dian Fossey was murdered in 1985 by unknown assailants.

Rwanda is blessed with extensive primeval forest and indigenous wildlife. This includes thirteen varieties of primate, three hundred types of birds and psychedelic turkeys! Unfortunately, when a large number of refugees who fled Rwanda in 1959/60 returned from Uganda in

1998, they came with thousands of long horned cattle. They passed through the game park causing a lot of damage, and even engaged in some poaching. Many of these cattle still graze in the park, degrading the natural habitat of the indigenous animals. The Ministry of Tourism is keen to turn this area back to a place where lions, leopards, giraffe, zebra, hippos, and all the different gazelles that dart around in large numbers through the scrubland, can be seen by Rwandans and tourists alike.

Cyangugu Diocese where Ken Barham concentrated much of his work is remote and has a large natural forest. In addition to the primates there are leopards, antelope and other small mammals. There were Pigmy elephants which Ken once videoed, but the conservation rangers found only the bones of one which had been killed.

Ken has organised many groups over the years from Britain and America to visit Rwanda. They travel mainly to see the ministry in which he is involved, but they were also keen to see some of the country, its amazing scenery and unique mountain gorillas. Invariably their enthusiastic verdict on returning back home, is that Rwanda is a most beautiful country. Ken's travellers are not just tourists. They see a side of Rwanda that most tourists only glimpse or even miss completely – the spiritual realities. As a result of civil war and the horrors of the Genocide, Rwanda was left devastated. Christians are in a unique position to support the people through prayer and fundraising.

Despite enjoying plentiful sunshine and rain, Rwanda struggles to feed its people. Because the country is heavily populated, the land is generally overworked and the steep slopes suffer continuously from soil erosion in the heavy rains that occur annually. Currently 56% of the population live below the poverty line.

The new government has removed all school fees for six years of primary and three years of secondary education, enabling all Rwanda's children to go to school. Health care is rudimentary, with three hundred qualified doctors serving a population of over nine million, and many die young from preventable disease. The government gives everyone a set sum of Medical Insurance enabling them to receive treatment in any registered hospital or clinic. AIDS is inevitably a big problem, made much worse by the mass rapes that were inflicted during the genocide.

Of course, tourism is a vital element in helping to provide the funds desperately needed for economic development, which will play a vital part in the continued healing of this beautiful, but wounded, nation.

*   *   *

For the previous half century, the Great Lakes region has seen a steady escalation of horror. In Rwanda, Burundi and in Zaire (now the Democratic Republic of Congo) many thousands have been massacred or violently raped. Powerful forces of evil lie behind all this and the Church needs to engage these forces with prayer, unity and reconciliation. Modern day solutions need to take into account the history of the people who have for centuries made this part of Africa their home.

The people of Rwanda are mainly three ancient ethnic groups. Hutus (88%), Tutsis (11%), and Twa pygmies (1%). These groups are often referred to as 'tribes'. However, a closer look shows us that they are better described as 'ethnic groups' because they do not fit the usual definition of a tribe. They all speak the same language, have done so for hundreds of years and they have the same culture. People groups in other African countries that are described as 'tribes' usually have their own language, traditional lands and tribal customs governing their lives. These will determine the conduct of weddings, funerals, rites of passage and a multitude of other ceremonies and life events. Tutsis and Hutus come from similar ancient Bantu origins and have lived together for centuries. Cultural and linguistic differences have been eroded with the passage of time to a point where there are none.

The Twa, also known as Batwa (which is the plural of Twa), are a pygmy people who were the oldest recorded inhabitants of the Great Lakes region of central Africa. Current populations are found in the states of Rwanda, Burundi, Uganda and the eastern portion of the Democratic Republic of Congo. In 2000, they numbered approximately 80,000 people, making them a significant minority group in these countries.

Traditionally, the Twa had been semi-nomadic hunter-gatherers and clay pot makers. They are the indigenous people of the mountain forests. Due to clearing of the forests for agriculture, logging, development projects, or creation of conservation areas, the Twa had been forced to leave these areas and establish new homes. As they seek to develop new means of sustaining their communities (such as agriculture and livestock development) most are currently landless and live in poverty. The ancestral land rights of the Twa had never been recognized by their governments and no compensation had been made for lands lost.

Twa children had little access to education, and their communities had limited representation in local and national government in the past. Due to their pygmy ancestry they suffered ethnic prejudice, discrimination, violence and general exclusion from society. Many Twa men struggled with alcoholism, known to occur in communities facing cultural collapse as men can no longer carry out traditional roles and provide for families. Prior to the nineteenth century, the three ethnic groups of Rwanda lived in relative harmony because their respective occupations of sedentary agriculture for the Hutu, and grazers for the Tutsi removed the need to compete.

Conceptions of the supposed ethnic groups in Rwanda have a long and complicated history. The definitions of 'Hutu' and 'Tutsi' peoples may have changed through time and location. Social structures were not identical throughout Rwanda, even during colonial times under the Belgian rule. The Tutsi aristocracy or elite was distinguished from Tutsi commoners, and wealthy Hutu were often indistinguishable from upper-class Tutsi. It was quite possible for a Hutu who obtained enough cows to be classified as a Tutsi.

When the Belgian colonialists conducted censuses, they wanted to identify the peoples throughout Rwanda-Burundi according to a simple classification scheme. They defined 'Tutsi' as anyone owning more than ten cows (a sign of wealth) or with the physical feature of the longer nose commonly associated with the Tutsi. The Europeans noticed that some Rwandans had noses they thought characteristic of Europeans, so they created historical and racial theories to explain why some Africans inherited such features. Early 20th-century Europeans believed the physical feature meant that some of the Tutsi had Caucasian or European ancestry. According to their racially based ideas, they thought the Tutsi were a 'superior' people of a primarily Horn of Africa or North African ancestry. Descent from Arabs of the Middle East was also suggested. In addition, some Tutsi believed they are descended from the ancient Israelites and have a mystical connection to Israel. The Europeans considered the majority Hutu to have the characteristics of the Bantu people of Central African and sub-Saharan origin.

Beginning about 1880, Catholic missionaries arrived in the African Great Lakes region. Later, when German forces occupied the area during World War 1, the conflict and efforts for Catholic conversion became more pronounced. As the Tutsi resisted conversion, the missionaries found success mainly among the Hutu. In an effort to reward conversion, the colonial government confiscated some traditionally Tutsi land and reassigned it to Hutus, igniting a conflict that has lasted into the 21st century.

In the Rwanda territory, from the 15th century until 1961, the people were ruled by a Tutsi king (the mwami). The Belgians abolished the monarchy in response to Hutu activism following the national referendum that led to independence. In the north-western area of the country (predominantly Hutu), by contrast, the society more closely resembled that of Bugandan society (in what is now Uganda); large regional landholders shared power instead of a central monarch.

Intermarriage between the two groups has not been uncommon. Hutu men often took Tutsi wives, although Tutsi men rarely married Hutu women. As traditionally the ethnicity of the father determined the status of the children, this contributed to the larger proportion of ethnic Hutu reported in the region. Many scholars have concluded that the determination of Tutsi was, and is, mainly an expression of class or caste, rather than ethnicity. DNA studies show clearly that the peoples are more closely related to each other as Bantu than to any other group. Differences have arisen due to social constructs, which created greater differences between the groups.

Colonial ineptness

Both Germany (before World War 1) and Belgium ruled the area in a colonial capacity. They believed in the racial superiority (a popular topic for Germans of that time) of the Tutsi. As a result, they allowed only the Tutsi to be educated or to participate in the colonial government. Since the Hutu were the majority, such discriminatory policies engendered resentment towards the Tutsi. When the Belgians assumed control following World War I, they continued the same policy of promoting the Tutsis.

The Belgians required the people to identify with a particular ethnic group by introducing compulsory ID cards for all Rwandans in 1931 which clearly stated if the person was Hutu or Tutsi. A differentiation between Hutu and Tutsi was vital to their 'divide and rule' strategy. Belgian colonialists viewed Africans in general as children who needed to be guided, but recognised the Tutsi as the ruling culture in 'Ruanda-Urundi'. In 1959, Belgium reversed its stance and allowed the majority Hutu to assume control of the government through universal elections.

This legacy of the one ethnic group striving for dominance over the other continued after independence (1st July 1962). As a result, ethnic conflict defined the relationship between Tutsis and Hutu until the Genocide of 1994, influencing most aspects of Rwandan society. An example was the education during the 1980s when school principals reported that although secondary school admissions were in accordance with quotas mandated by the Habyarimana government (in line with the proportions of the groups within the country), and by competition within ethnic groups, the students of Tutsi origin (14% of intake) on average were a disproportionately large percentage (nearly 50%) of those who graduated. This result provoked accusations of ethnic favouritism. It may have been a product of the often wealthier Tutsi not needing their children's labour to contribute to family welfare and therefore being able to stay in school long enough to graduate.

CHAPTER FIVE

Genocide Perpetrated

The senior politicians and military officers that planned the Genocide had one other weapon at their disposal; one that was far more sophisticated than machetes or clubs. It was a weapon without which they could not have perpetrated their crimes as efficiently as they did. A weapon particularly suited to the African context in which it was used – *the radio.*

Compared with the developed world, relatively few Africans can afford to own a television or even have electricity in their homes to power one. In contrast to this, many own a battery-powered transistor radio, or know a friend, relation or neighbour who owns one. You don't even have to be able to read. This fact makes the radio the most powerful instrument of mass communication in most of sub-Saharan Africa, and Rwanda was no different. *Radio Télévision Libre des Mille Collines* (RTLM) began to broadcast from July 8th 1993 and continued until July 31st 1994. The station's name is French for 'One Thousand Hills Free Radio and Television', deriving from the popular description of Rwanda as *'Land of a Thousand Hills'.* It received support from the government controlled Radio Rwanda, which initially allowed it to transmit using their equipment. As the Genocide was taking place, the United States military drafted a plan to jam RTLM's broadcasts, but this action was never taken because of the cost of the operation and the legal implications of interfering with Rwanda's sovereignty. Such caution on their part seems to have evaporated as a national policy in more recent days!

The part played by the broadcasts cannot be overstated. The sole aim was to stir up hatred against the Tutsis, a task in which it was spectacularly successful. It also targeted moderate Hutus, the UN, the peace talks and Belgians. It was widely listened to by the general population because it cleverly mixed the racial propaganda with sophisticated use of humour and popular Zairian music. It particularly attracted vulnerable youth to its cause, and many of these made up the militant Interahamwe militia. The Tutsis also listened to it avidly – for a very different reason – and with mounting fear.

It developed its own language of hatred and everyone hearing it understood the meaning of the code phrases. Tutsis were constantly referred to as Inyenzi (cockroaches) or Inzoka (snakes). The broadcasts frequently urged the groups of killers to 'Do your work,' or 'Do your duty.' Their work was murder, torture, rape and robbery, aimed at nothing less than ridding the country of all Tutsis. The rhetoric built upon pre-existing animosities and prejudices between the Hutu and Tutsi populations.

One observer reported seeing hundreds of Tutsis fleeing their villages with 'just the clothes on their backs and a transistor radio pressed to their ear.' The broadcasts even helped to coordinate the activity of the Interahamwe gangs by informing them of places the Tutsi had fled to in large numbers.

With the atmosphere set for Genocide, one event triggered the start of the killing. Rwanda's President Habyarimana was returning to Kigali on April 6th 1994 in his private Falcon 50 aircraft from Arusha in Tanzania where he had signed the peace agreement. His first task on his return was announced in advance, and that was to be signing into Rwanda law the Arusha Accords. Burundi's

President Cyprian Ntaryamira (also a Hutu) was also in the plane on his way back home. It was early evening and already dark as the plane approached Kigali airport when it was shot down by what is thought to be a SAM 6 missile attack from the ground.

Whether this was the pre-planned event designed to create an excuse to begin the Genocide, or just an opportunity that was taken, is not clear. The majority of observers think it was the former. There is also divided opinion on who perpetrated the attack. The hate radio immediately blamed the RPF army. 'The cockroaches have killed our President' was the cry. In the unlikely event that the RPF possessed such a sophisticated weapon, it is difficult to see how they could have transported it to the heart of the government-held area unchallenged. The SAM 6 system is large enough to require a truck to move it. The RPF and many other observers blame extremist Hutus in the Rwandan government for the attack. Their alleged motive was that President Habyarimana had signed the peace treaty and they had no intention of allowing the Tutsis to share power. They viewed the President as soft on the Tutsis; he would never have the courage to deal effectively with them.

To shoot down an aircraft in the dark – it was 9.00 pm in the evening – requires a weapon of some sophistication and trained operators. It had to be the military of one side or the other. Untrained irregular militia who were typically young and drunk a lot of the time, seem to be unlikely candidates. One witness to the events has even blamed the French, operating at the instigation of the Hutu extremists for the attack. Impartial opinions are difficult to acquire and for the time being, there is no definitive proof of who was responsible.

One thing is certain; this was the event that triggered the nightmare of the next hundred days. What began in

Kigali quickly spread to the rest of the country, thanks to the radio which continuously urged the killers on to further atrocities. The army was also involved using small arms such as pistols and rifles. Part of the preparation had been to list the names and addresses of as many Tutsis as could be found. The military went from house to house with their lists, killing and raping as they went. Meanwhile, the radio continued urging the Interahamwe militia to 'Do your work.' The radio called for 'a final war to exterminate the Tutsis.' Emboldened by the actions of the army, the Interahamwe now knew that they could kill without inhibition. No one was going to call them to account; the government itself was leading the way. Within hours, road blocks were set up throughout most of the country to stop Tutsis from escaping. The same road blocks frequently became killing grounds.

The Tutsis who had no transport fled to churches or schools to try to defend themselves by locking doors or throwing stones. Some mistakenly thought that the churches might be a sanctuary. The hate radio even told them to go to schools and churches to be safe. Too late the Tutsis realised that this was inevitably a trap. Churches were invaded; even clergy and nuns were not safe from the Interahamwe thugs. Most shockingly, some Hutu clergy even sided with the Interahamwe and gave up their Tutsi members.

Many Tutsis tried to hide but few escaped by this means for long. The need for food and water for themselves or crying babies eventually revealed their hiding places. No one was spared. Men, women and children were all massacred. Babies were wrenched from their mothers' arms to be dashed against rocks or walls or mercilessly slashed with the ubiquitous machetes. Some children were forced to watch their parents being brutally tortured, before being killed themselves. Others were drowned in rivers. Victims were sometimes forced to kill their loved ones. Both Hutu and Tutsi mothers were forced to kill their own Tutsi children.

The Interahamwe tended to recruit mostly among the poor. As soon as they went into action, they drew around them a rag-tag militia of even poorer people. They were the street boys, rag-pickers, car-washers and homeless unemployed. For these young men the genocide was seen as the best thing that could ever happen to them. They had the blessings of the Hutu government and the army to take revenge on socially powerful people as long as they were on the wrong side of the ethnic divide. They could steal, rape and kill with minimum justification and get drunk for free. The political aims pursued by the masters of this evil jamboree were quite beyond their scope. They just went along, knowing it would not last. Did they think of future consequences? It is in the nature of African culture to live for today and not worry much about tomorrow.

Unique in the history of Genocides was the involvement of women. They were just as eager to kill. Women inflicted unspeakable cruelty on other women. Victims' genitals were mutilated with machetes, knives, and other implements. Women killed babies without mercy. It was common for several Interahamwe to kill one person. It was the policy to implicate as many people as possible. Female victims who survived were often mass-raped resulting in a large proportion of them becoming HIV positive along with the babies that were born later.

Ken and Jill watched in vain the television news hoping to hear something specific about their own centre of ministry in Cyangugu, but the remoteness of the area meant that the spotlight of news – limited as it was – focused on the main cities such as Kigali. However, Cyangugu's remoteness was no protection. The preparations for the Genocide and the chilling efficiency of the hate radio broadcasts ensured that the killing broke out in every part of the country not controlled by the RPF, more or less simultaneously.

Subsequent investigations of the Genocide have sadly confirmed that many Hutu church members and even some of the Catholic priests supported the Interahamwe. However, this shocking aspect of the killing was not universal. In Bweyeye, close to the border with Burundi and one of the three parishes that make up the Cyangugu diocese, a different story can be told. Even in this border region the church congregation were soon alerted that the Interahamwe had come to kill with alarming promptness. The target was their Pastor Azaria Ndizihiwe and his wife Ruth. Ruth was clearly a Tutsi from her appearance. She was heavily pregnant and ready to give birth at any time. Unfortunately, as elsewhere, being pregnant was no protection for mother or baby. When the Interahamwe arrived the Christians of the parish, who were mostly Hutu, acted quickly to protect Ruth. They rescued her and took Ruth and her children through the forest where she promptly gave birth to a son whom they named Erenesti. Mother and baby both survived the traumatic circumstances of the birth and Erenesti has grown into a healthy young man.

Later the same day, the Interahamwe, having had Ruth snatched from their grasp by the Christians, returned to kill Pastor Azaria. He was just about to make his escape on his motorcycle to join Ruth and the children, when the thugs caught him and held him with a machete to his throat. Azaria was not clearly a Tutsi or a Hutu, like many in Rwanda, he was of indeterminate appearance. Nevertheless, whatever he was, being married to a Tutsi was considered enough of a sin to warrant his murder. Once again the members of his congregation courageously intervened to protect him. They hustled him away to join his family and newborn son, leaving the killers with the consolation prize of the valuable motorbike. Ken had bought the motorcycle for Azaria with a grant from Tearfund. Apart from their Genocidal activities, the Interahamwe were also thieves and grabbed anything of value from their victims and their homes. The motorcycle was later recovered.

Ken himself refers – with some hesitation – to an account of a notorious incident in a technical school in southern Rwanda. This happened in Murambi, a district in southern Rwanda not far from the city of Butare. The local Tutsis all ran to the church hoping for protection. The Catholic Bishop and the Mayor (who pretended to be on their side) told them it wasn't safe in the church and that it would be better for them to go to the vacant technical school on the hill, where they would be protected by the French army in the area.

Consequently, ten days into the Genocide – on April 16, 1994 – an incredible 65,000 Tutsis ran there for protection, but the whole thing was a set-up. No sooner had they settled in, the electricity and water supply was disconnected, and for the next week they had nothing but contaminated water to drink and no food. Then they were attacked by bands of random killers but managed to fend them off with stones. But then, a few nights later on April 21, the killing started with a vengeance. The French soldiers who said they would protect them, disappeared and in their place came local Hutu Interahamwe armed with machetes and a battalion of policemen (gendarmes) sent by Colonel Bagosora – a mastermind in the Genocide.

All hell broke loose and unprecedented bloodshed occurred that night. 15,000 managed to run through the hills to a church a few miles away, only to be discovered the next day and slaughtered en masse. Meanwhile, at the school, 45,000 Tutsis were dead. Only twenty escaped and four were left for dead and lay under bodies until the killing was over.

The school is now a Genocide Memorial. The various rooms of this school are filled with skeletons that have been preserved intact with lime. The tattered clothing of some still clings to the bones. The skeletons often show evidence of the mortal wounds and injuries that were inflicted on them. April 7th is Memorial Day each year and Ken attended one of these at the former school, at which President Kagame and a number of his ministers were present. The President made one of the speeches. Some of the survivors of that incident also spoke and told of their horror at seeing some of the French soldiers playing volleyball on the graves of people who had been killed. This incident is so bizarre it is unlikely to have been made up. The remains of 55,000 people were buried in the immediate vicinity of the former school.

Many of the Tutsis hoped that the small, but well armed UN force would give them some protection; but in one of the most shameful episodes in the United Nation's chequered history, they refused to get involved. They insisted that their mandate only allowed them to 'monitor the peace.' After a number of UN troops had been brutally killed, they soon had the order to evacuate.

The French

If the French intervention in this tragedy was a belated attempt to end the killing, it was an abject failure! On June 22, with no sign of UN deployment taking place, the Security

Council authorized French forces to land in Bukavu, Zaire, on a *humanitarian mission*. They deployed throughout southwest Rwanda in an area they called 'Zone Turquoise', supposedly quelling the Genocide and stopping the fighting there, but often arriving in areas only after 'Genocidaires' (Interahamwe) had killed Tutsi citizens. 'Operation Turquoise' was later accused of aiding the Hutu army against the RPF by Jacques Bihozagara who was then Rwandan ambassador to France. He later testified, 'Operation Turquoise' was aimed only at protecting Genocide perpetrators, because the Genocide continued even within the Turquoise zone.'

Many observers suspect that the motives of the French President François Mitterrand, were at best mixed and at worst sinister. Their force landed at Bukavu, which is across the southern shores of Lake Kivu in the DCR (Congo) and set up a military base there. It can be argued that what Rwanda really needed at that time was a strongly armed and independent police force. Heavy weapons are hardly needed to subdue a rag tag militia armed with machetes, clubs and the occasional pistol, often under the influence of looted alcohol! Instead, the French treated it as a full military operation with heavy weapons, ready to fight a conventional battle. Presumably, the French thought they had some responsibility to act in this French speaking part of Africa. The first action of the French military was to establish a 'Cordon Sanitaire' in the southern part of Rwanda.

The present Rwandan government and many of the survivors of the Genocide take a very dim view of the French force's response to the crisis. Analysis of documents subsequently released from the Paris archive of former president Francois Mitterrand show how the Rwandan Patriotic Front invasion was considered as clear aggression by an Anglophone neighbour on a Francophone country. The documents are said to argue that the RPF was a part of an 'Anglophone plot', involving the President of Uganda, to create an English-speaking 'Tutsi-land' and increase Anglophone influence at the expense of French influence. It is claimed that the policy of France was to avoid a military victory by the RPF. If these records are true – and there is no reason to believe that they are not – President Mitterand's naïve and self-serving reaction to the crisis, is shocking.

Following an investigation of the plane crash of 6 April 1994 that killed both the Rwandan President Juvenal Habyarimana and Burundian President Cyprien Ntaryamira, precipitating the Genocide, the French judge Jean-Louis Bruguiere indicted eight associates of Rwandan president Paul Kagame on November 17th 2006. President Kagame himself was not indicted, as he had immunity under French law as a head of state. President Kagame denied the allegations, decrying them as politically motivated and broke off diplomatic relationships with France in November 2006. He then ordered the formation of a commission of his own Rwandan Justice Ministry's employees which was officially 'charged with assembling proof of the involvement of France in the genocide'.

Findings of the commission were released on Kagame's order on August 5, 2008. They accused the French government of knowing of preparations for the Genocide and helping to train the ethnic Hutu militia members. They also named thirty-three senior French military and political officials of involvement in the Genocide. A statement accompanying the release claimed that 'French soldiers themselves were directly involved in assassinations of Tutsis and Hutus accused of hiding Tutsis.' A BBC report commented that French Foreign Minister, Bernard Kouchner denied French responsibility in connection with the Genocide but admitted that 'political errors had been made.'

The suspicions about United Nations and French policies in Rwanda between 1990 and 1994 and allegations that France supported the Hutus led to the creation of a French Parliamentary Commission on Rwanda, which published its report on December 15, 1998. In particular, Francois-Xavier Verschave, former president of the French NGO Survie, which accused the French army of protecting the Hutus during the Genocide, was instrumental in establishing this Parliamentary commission. The commission released its final report on December 15, 1998. It documented 'ambiguities and confusion' in both the French and UN responses.

As the world has so often seen, political point scoring frequently takes priority and makes the search for truth much more difficult. Once again in conflict, the first casualty has been the truth! Both sides hurl exaggerated charges at the other. What is more clear and accepted by most of neutral observers is that the role of the French was ambiguous and unhelpful at best. Truth may be 'the first casualty of war', but in this case, the piled skeletal remains of the dead bear compelling witness to the horrific events that took place in this school and the surrounding 'Cordon Sanitaire'.

As soon as the national situation became clear, the Rwanda Patriotic Front, under the command of Paul Kagame went on the offensive with renewed urgency. The RPF struck southward towards Kigali, while at the same time a force swung clockwise to capture the countryside. Kigali fell to RPF forces on 4 July, allowing the freed-up forces to capture the last remaining stronghold of Gisenyi, in the northwest, on 18 July. In the south-west of the country, French forces from 'Operation Turquoise' controlled a large area, allowing the Hutu to cross over to Zaire. The area was given over to UN control on 21 August 1994, thus giving the RPF complete control of the country.

By now, the hate radio had transferred to a mobile operation which continued broadcasting as they fled the advancing RPF force. The radio told the country that they were still in Kigali and that the capital was still under Hutu control; a pretence that they could only keep up until the end of July, but certainly accounted for further Tutsi deaths.

When Ken was finally able to return to Cyangugu in September 1994, the Ethiopian UN soldiers were in charge, followed by the Ghanaians, but the RPF had won the country. It was an Ethiopian soldier who tried to stop Ken taking a photo of what was left of his house!

Remains of Ken's House. September 1994

There is little doubt that without the military intervention of the RPF, the Hutu extremists would have largely achieved their aim. Few Tutsis would have survived to tell their horrific stories. As it was, by the time the RPF had gained control of the whole country, more than half the Tutsi population had tragically been killed. Later when the numbers were estimated, it was clear that the rate of killing was about three times that of the Nazi death camps of the Second World War combined.

Of their own free will, men and women opened their souls to become the instruments of hell. Behind the scenes the military and extremist members of the government were pulling the strings, but what they didn't perhaps realise, was that they themselves had surrendered their will to evil forces whose only agenda was to use them to accomplish cruelty and premature death.

When it became clear that the RPF was going to take control of Kigali, over a million Hutu fled the country. The largest group by far crossed into Zaire and massive refugee camps were established. Many of the Interahamwe, with some of their leaders infiltrated the refugee camps. In fact they set up quasi administrations in the camps and continued to oppress even their own people. From these camps, numerous raids into Rwanda were organised after the Genocide was over.

The Hutus understandably expected massive reprisals by the new Tutsi government. There were some reprisal killings carried out locally, but nowhere near what was feared and certainly not promoted by the new government. Once the interim government was firmly in control, law and order was established. The Rwandan government and the International Criminal Court have worked hard to bring the perpetrators to justice for their crimes. Some have been tried and sentenced; others fled to the camps. Others were able to flee further to live anonymously in other parts of Africa, Europe or North America with the looted resources that they had gained.

There will however, be one final court of justice that none will be able to evade. This will be the final judgement at which God Himself will preside on the day when all the records will be revealed and the deeds of everyone – including the Interahamwe and their political leaders – will be judged.

Jesus, give us faith to follow
Through affliction, pain and toil,
In the dangerous times of plenty
Keep us faithful, true and loyal.

John Young

CHAPTER SIX

Boarding School

In 1945, and while still only nine years old, Ken went to Kenya to boarding school at The Hill School, Eldoret and then to Kenton College, Nairobi. At the age of twelve he enrolled at the Duke of York School, in Nairobi, where the atmosphere was very different from anything Ken had encountered so far in his young life. There were only a few boys from Christian families. In an attempt to retain the Christian lifestyle and standards of their homes, the Christian boys gathered early in the mornings to read the Scripture Union portion and pray. Back in the dormitory the other boys mocked and bullied Ken because of his Christian faith. They humiliated him by making him sing. Under this pressure, the group stopped their morning prayers. Ken always felt a little ashamed about this. The power of peer pressure, so often talked about in our day, is certainly not a new problem. Like most boys, Ken wanted to be popular with his mates. He drifted into a rather bad group of boys who flouted almost any school rule. He became very keen on reading 'Westerns' by Zane Gray and sometimes would even read a book during history and maths lessons!

In those days, Ken and most of the boys bore no grudge at being punished for breaking the rules. If you were caught, 'six of the best' from the headmaster was expected. It was perfectly normal, and to show their bravado, the boys would say 'Thank you, sir' as they left the Head's office.

By the end of his third year the headmaster decided that he had to take action; writing to all the parents of this gang to say that they could finish their School Certificate, but would then have to leave the school. Ken was a year younger than the rest of the gang so he had an extra year. His parents were in England when they received the headmaster's letter. For them, this was a family crisis.

His mother flew out to Kenya and came to the school in Aunt Mary Leakey's Morris Minor. She told Ken that when his father read the letter, saying the headmaster had hoped for better from a clergyman's son, his father wept. He had never known his father cry and it hurt him deeply. He had never felt such shame. For some, sending their young child away to boarding school for months at a time is inconceivable. We must not think that parents of that time didn't have the same emotional attachment to their children as they have today. Your child must have a good education and this was the only way to achieve it. It was part of the sacrifice that missionaries made when they went to serve God in remote and often dangerous places.

Another experience at school that had contrasted sharply with Ken's very peaceful and Christian home life was the habit of the colonial boys to refer to black Kenyans as 'Wogs'. They called them by this derogatory name because most of them resented the fact that Africans were being given the same education as they were. Ken was shocked and offended that fine people like William Majoro or his best friend Enoch Mihigo should be called by that offensive term. Knowing how the Kenyan colonials treated the Africans, Ken was not surprised when, during his time at the school the 'Mau Mau' anti-Colonial movement began in Kenya. They were mainly the fiercely proud Kikuyu people and they took oaths to kill Europeans. The conflict set the stage for Kenyan independence on 12th December 1963.

The term 'wogs' has, for a long time, been a derogatory term used for people of a darker skin than Europeans.

There are a variety of theories about the origin of the word; some of them rather fanciful. Probably the most convincing one is that it was a convenient acronym that originated in British-controlled Egypt towards the end of the nineteenth century and spread to other parts of the Empire. It was not meant to be offensive then as it is today. It simply stood for 'Worker On Government Service', and if anything, it was complimentary because it indicated a position of trust and status.

Ken's emotional and spiritual trauma over the way he had caused grief to his parents had a beneficial effect. He completely reformed, broke with the gang and concentrated on sport, his studies and improving his behaviour. The change was dramatic. The school was so impressed with his transformation, that Ken was appointed as head boy of the new 'Thompson House' – a reward and an honour. It shouldn't be overlooked that this new role had been given to Ken not just because of his new start, but also because he showed the personal qualities and leadership attributes that were required. In his last three years at school he won the 440 yards in athletics, earning him the school colours, which he also won in Rugby (Vice Captain) and Soccer (Captain). He also participated in school drama and musical productions.

He loved his parents very much and was ashamed of letting them down and from that point on he was determined to give his very best in everything he did. Thus in his final Higher School Certificate year he was appointed Head Boy of the school, a tremendous achievement given his earlier setback. Best of all, he was now a fine Christian example to the other boys in the school. Only God knows the full impact that he had on the other boys, but he can point to one of his contemporaries who converted to Christianity as a result of his new witness and example. This friend went on into ministry and became a vicar in the Church of England, The Revd. Christopher Carey.

Sundays at the Duke of York School, Nairobi, could be boring. The school bus took anyone who wanted to go to 8.00am Communion at the Cathedral. This meant they could miss the morning service in the school chapel. In the afternoon the school bus took boys to the 'Crusader' class in Nairobi, run by a group of Christian doctors with separate classes for boys and girls. The classes contained pupils from the Duke of York, the Prince of Wales and the Kenya High School.

One Sunday Dr Calcott, who ran the boys' group, asked Ken to take his car and go to Dr Jarvis' house and get some more cakes. Mrs Jarvis made hundreds of small iced cakes for tea after the class. He told Ken to take his Ford Zephyr and handed him the keys. Ken's heart 'skipped a beat' at this exciting prospect. Ken could drive well enough, but aged seventeen, to drive this six-cylinder 2,262cc car on his own was very special. At the time it was the biggest car Ford made in Britain and it was built like a tank.

He felt very privileged and even rather proud of himself as he parked outside the Jarvis house and obtained the cakes that were needed. As he started the engine to return there was an admiring crowd of girl Crusaders watching! The six cylinders purred smoothly, but the steering column gearshift would not go in into first gear. Feeling embarrassed and crestfallen, Ken had to go back into the house and report his failure. Elizabeth Jarvis came out, opened the bonnet, pressed the gear connection, shut the bonnet and told him to put it into gear. It went in easily and he drove off, his pride having taken a tumble. However, the experience did nothing to minimise the gratitude Ken felt for this eye specialist, Doug Calcott, who gave up every Sunday afternoon to influence boys from a tough boarding school to live for Jesus Christ. His influence did not end with Kenya, his friendship and professional expertise were to be an important factor in Ken's later life.

With hindsight, we can see, even in these early formative years that Ken was developing into a person who would never be content with the ordinary or doing the minimum required, in whatever field of work or aspect of life he found himself, he always wanted to do more, multi-function, grasp opportunities that came along and explore the possibilities. Little did he know it in those school days, but he was being prepared for a life of service that he might never have imagined. God had plans for him!

Cruelty

In 1951 at the age of fifteen, during one of the school holidays, Ken had his first experience of how brutal the Belgian colonial rule could be at Ngozi in what is now Burundi. With his two brothers and two sisters, he lived in a mission bungalow. Their missionary parents were busy teaching clergy and their wives. They had a cook (Karekezi), a houseboy (Ndabanogeye), and a man who looked after them during the day (William Majoro). They were all local Africans and lived on the compound.

The African theological students would come into their house and sing hymns every Sunday night and felt free to wander in at any other time. The doors were never locked and the children had complete freedom to build camps in the woods below the houses and play in the grassy hillside. The 'mission station' was the whole hill on which the only two cars were theirs and the local doctor's. Being the eldest son, Ken was the first one that his father allowed to drive the car, as soon as he was tall enough to see the road from the driver's seat. By the age of twelve Ken was a competent driver, and passed his driving test with the Belgian Administrator when he was sixteen.

One day during a school holiday, Ken drove to the small town of Ngozi about five miles away to see the Belgian District Commissioner. On arriving at the District Office Ken was horrified to see him punishing a line of local African men by laying into them with a rhino hide whip, tearing into their flesh. They knelt on the floor with their hands tied behind their backs. Ken was deeply shocked and left as fast as he could. He never found out the reason for this cruel treatment, but the awful vision of it has stayed with him to this day.

This incident which Ken inadvertently witnessed, unfortunately was far from isolated in colonial Africa. The very fact that this could happen one hundred and forty years after Britain abolished slavery, illustrated that the attitude many Europeans still had to the African, left much to be desired. For Ken, it stood in stark contrast to high regard that his own Christian missionary parents had for the Africans that God had called them to love and serve. For Ken it was an early lesson in a life that God planned for him. A life in which he learned to value all men as God does and see them as souls that God loves unconditionally.

CHAPTER SEVEN

Ranching In Africa

After gaining the Higher School Certificate, Ken went to England with the promise of a place to study medicine at St Bartholomew's Hospital, London. He found the high standards of the medical studies very difficult. Ken had not inherited the academic brilliance of his father. Though he did his best and worked hard, it became clear that he was not going to make it as a doctor. The Dean very kindly suggested that it was going to be a struggle for him and it might be good to take some other course. Ken was disappointed but not surprised. With hindsight it is clear that Ken's gifts lay in other areas.

He was then offered a job on the Namutamba Tea Estate and Dairy Farm with Malcolm and Barbara Lea-Wilson, in Uganda. This farm was one of the centres of the East African revival. People came to visit from all over the world to see what God was doing. Daily meetings were held there. Malcolm and Barbara knew Ken's father and although they had not met Ken, they knew about his situation. It was through this connection that Ken was offered the job on the farm.

Consequently, in 1957 aged twenty one, Ken flew out to Uganda to take up this offer. At Namutamba, Malcolm had developed the work that his father had founded and he had built up a large herd of local cows. Most of them were on a ranch twenty-five miles away, but there was a herd of one hundred within the tea estate in a series of paddocks. A pickup was sent in to Kampala daily with milk and mail, but the operation ran at a considerable loss. The cows just didn't produce enough milk. Malcolm asked Ken to try and make it profitable through better milk production. After research and experiment, Ken and Malcolm concluded that they would need to bring in some 'exotic' cows. At that time there were no such cows in Uganda, so to improve the milk yield from the farms the colonial government decided to import and supply Guernsey calves to suitable farms.

Namutamba farm and the Gayaza Girls School seventeen miles north of the Ugandan capital of Kampala, were two of the places chosen. Gayaza School was founded in 1905 by Christian missionaries, whose intention was to educate girls based on a strong Christian foundation. They realised that one of the best ways of developing Christianity in the community was by having Christian mothers in whose care children spent all their formative years. The curriculum included cultivation, handwork, child-care, needlework, scripture, reading, writing, arithmetic and geography. Gayaza School had a fraternal link with Sherborne School for girls in the U.K. Gayaza school survives to this day as the oldest girls' school in Uganda and is still a place of excellence for girls to be educated.

Both centres were given calves to rear. They were fed calf pellets impregnated with antibiotics. The dietary supplement and the antibiotics were supposed to ensure bigger, fatter cows and overcome the problem of a tick-borne disease called 'East Coast Fever'. This disease caused the glands in the neck to swell and the animal could die in a matter of hours.

Gayaza succeeded better than Namutamba did because its calves still died. It was obvious that they needed to concentrate on dealing with the ticks. An automatic spray system with a diesel engine pumping anti-tick spray

(Coopertox) onto the cows as they walked through a crush was set up. The excess liquid drained back into the tank and circulated again so the whole herd could be sprayed fairly quickly. They kept a herd of one hundred local cows in paddocks and sprayed them twice a week until there were no ticks visible on the cattle. They double fenced these paddocks, situated within the fields of tea and cultivated the twelve-foot space between the fences. This protected the inner paddock containing the cows from animal-born ticks because the ticks had no means of crossing the cultivated strip.

On one visit to Kyanamugera ranch in 1958, they had arranged for a government vet to visit them there to inoculate the two thousand head of cattle. He was an Englishman fresh out from the UK, knowing nothing about Africa. He arrived at midday and Ken told him that the cattle were not anywhere near as they had all gone for pasture and water, which they would need in the midday sun. Ken told him 'I can't show you any cattle, but I can show you some elephants!'

The herdsmen had said that elephants had destroyed some of the fences and were causing chaos with some of the crops. He then told him to bring his camera. They piled into the farm lorry and set off to the corner of the ranch where the elephants had been reported. On arrival, one of the men climbed a large ant hill and whispered 'They are here!' Half the party went one way and Ken and the vet went the other and climbed into a tree. Sure enough, half a dozen elephants were heading their way. He was told that he would never see wild elephants this close again. As the huge creatures approached the tree the vet dropped his camera lens. Ken shinned down, picked it up and got back just as they got right up to the tree. They kept very still hoping the elephants couldn't see them. The other party started *'ululating'*. The elephants flapped their big ears and ambled off in that direction, so Ken and the vet scrambled down and got back to the lorry. Ken never saw the photos!

They heard later that the vet had asked if he could buy the Royal Drums from the King's palace. This caused a cultural offence and he was expelled from the country!

Every week a lorry went from the farm to the main herd twenty five miles away to take food for the herdsmen and bring back firewood for the tea factory. It was part of Ken's duties to drive the lorry on this trip. Malcolm went with him the first time to show him round. Malcolm asked him to drive as much as possible without the foot brake, using the gears for reducing speed on corners and hills. With five tons on board the brakes worked very hard on this very hilly road. This was a safer way to drive in the conditions and preserved the brakes from premature wear.

The usual task for the day was to hear reports from the herdsmen about births, sickness or death in the herd and discuss solutions. Of course they were the experts, but Ken was the boss (on behalf of Malcolm). Another task was to sell selected stock to cattle dealers, and this would take most of the day. These were Muslim butchers whose customers would only eat meat slaughtered by them facing Mecca according to Halal tradition. The herdsmen would first advise Ken of the real value of the animal. He would then receive an offer from the dealers which, of course, would be far too low. To show his disgust at this derisory offer, Ken would walk off saying they were just playing. He would do some other work to show he was not interested. When they approached again his price would come down a bit and they would come up a bit until everyone reached somewhere near the real price. The bartering always took hours and occasionally they wouldn't agree, but usually the day ended with a few cattle sold for the right price. Of course, this bartering ritual is expected and normal, not just in Africa, but throughout most of the developing world. Only naïve tourists pay the first asking price.

Ken was sent to Kenya to spend some months studying dairy management and learning to judge Jersey cows. He lived on a dairy farm with Charles Moore, one of the judges of Jerseys at the agricultural shows in Kenya. Here Ken had a valuable opportunity to learn about Jerseys from an expert. He bought six heifers in calf and took them back to Uganda on the train from Nairobi to Kampala. It was a new experience for these handsome ladies. The farm lorry then took them from the station to the farm. The local cows in the paddocks were then gradually replaced as soon as the Jerseys calved. They were very lucky to have five of the six cows produce heifers and all six flourished. These six Jersey cows produced more milk than a hundred local cows! They were beautiful and Ken thoroughly enjoyed working with them. Forty years after he left the farm he still gets a thrill whenever he sees a Jersey cow!

*   *   *

A call to ministry

Although Ken was there to manage the dairy herd, in his spare time he was also involved in ministry to the local community. On Sundays at the Namutamba Tea Estate he went with a Rwandan member of staff John Bunyenyezi, who worked in the dairy section, to neighbouring tea estates where thousands of Rwandans worked and where a short service would be held for them. Ken played a piano accordion (he admits not very expertly) and John Bunyenyezi led some prayers. John later trained for the ministry. Ken spoke the language of the Rwandans and was able to minister to them in their mother tongue. It is a great advantage to be able to speak the local language in Africa and his upbringing gave him the ability to speak several.

One day a neighbour, William Nagenda, who was one of the leading men in the Revival and who at this time was travelling to many parts of the world as an evangelist, came and spoke to Ken as he was putting in a new fence post. He asked him about his future and stated that he was sure Ken should be ordained in the Anglican ministry. Ken told him that all his life people had said 'I expect you will follow in your father's footsteps,' or words to this effect. His reply to William was that he was very happy on the farm. He liked his job, liked his cows and the little cottage where he lived. He had a cook, a house boy, and free milk and eggs from the farm. He liked his two co-workers and got on well with them. It was an idyllic life as far as Ken was concerned in the Africa he knew and loved, with a revival going on at that time, and he didn't want to be a clergyman!

John Bunyenyezi and William Nagenda were studying at the theological college in Kampala when the Revival was spreading. Their high standard of holiness and their fervency for Christ made the college authorities uncomfortable and they were expelled. The college considered this moving of God as rather extreme.

William however, was sure that God wanted Ken to train for Anglican ministry. Ken, who had great respect for William, replied that God would have to make it very plain to him that becoming a clergyman was what He wanted him to do. William wasn't so easily put off. 'What sort of sign do you expect, a voice from the sky?' he said. 'The trouble with you is that you are not willing!' Ken finally agreed to ask the Lord to guide him and make it very clear if He wanted him to be ordained.

When a great revival leader tells you that he is *sure* that you should do a particular thing, it is wise to see if he is right and test the calling. To do this, Ken left the farm for a visit to England, leaving all his possessions and belongings in the cottage, not wanting to pre-judge the outcome of his visit, even though he still felt that he didn't want to be a clergyman. Having been challenged in this way by William though, he wanted to settle the issue and see if he should pursue this path. Once he was home, he applied for a candidates' selection course, which was held at a retreat centre in St. Albans.

On their first night at St Albans, the candidates took it in turn to introduce themselves and talk about where they had come from and why they wanted to be ordained. In his brief introduction Ken said his father was a clergyman, but he knew that that didn't make him a Christian. He explained that he had accepted Christ as his personal Saviour and he wanted to know if God wanted him to serve Him as a clergyman rather than a farmer.

The following morning, at the first of several interviews the Canon, who was from Croydon, asked him to repeat what he had said about his father, which he did. He made it clear to Ken that he thought that what he had said was wrong. If Ken had been baptized in the church, *he was made a Christian*. Ken argued that he had been 'born again' and that is what made him a Christian. At the end of this interview Ken said, *'If I have to believe that to be ordained, please count me out.'*

The other interviews were mostly talking about Jersey cows, double fencing, East Coast Fever, and all the things that he had been involved with in Uganda. Ken rather assumed that this was the end of his application. He was quite taken aback when he received a letter two weeks later from the Bishop of Southwark informing him, 'You will be pleased to know that the committee have recommended you for training for the ministry.' The conditions were that he should enrol at a theological college and find the fees.

The conditions were a challenge, but Ken needed a clear sign, and if God could provide the college and the fees, then that would be his answer. God did provide. He applied to Clifton Theological College, Bristol. This college was started in 1932 in Stoke House as an offshoot of Tyndale Hall of the Bible Churchmens' Missionary Society (BCMS – now called Crosslinks). Clifton continued until 1971 when it joined Tyndale Hall and the women's college, Dalton House, to form Trinity College. Clifton offered him a place, even though term had just started. He also applied to the Church's Board for Ministry, who agreed to give him a grant for training. Consequently, he wrote to Malcolm Lea-Wilson at Namutamba and informed him that he wasn't coming back; he was going to commence training for the Anglican ministry. Some may have said that it was inevitable, but Ken knew in his own heart that he wasn't just following in his father's footsteps; he had heard God's call on his life and was following it. He had no way of knowing then how important this step would prove to be for the long-term ministry that God had planned for him.

Saviour, give us strength to follow
Your example and your law:
Loving You above all others,
Others may we love the more.

John Young, (at Clifton)

CHAPTER EIGHT

Early Ministry

Ken completed the first year of training successfully, working long hours, with a quick game of squash daily for exercise. In the long summer vacation, he had the opportunity to visit Canada. He found a job in Toronto for the first month, cleaning TV tubes with hydrofluoric acid, to help with his finances. The rest of the time he was a counsellor at Ontario Pioneer Camp in Muskoka on Lake Clearwater. In addition to looking after five seventeen year old boys in his tent, he learnt to water-ski. It was great entertainment for the boys to watch the counsellors falling off their skis as they learnt!

Back in Bristol, the Principal asked him to be Deputy Senior Student with Tony Baker. His leadership abilities had become evident to the college. Ken, impatient to return to Uganda as a missionary, asked the Principal if he could try to complete the last two years in one and he agreed. Well motivated, he worked hard, attended more lectures and managed to complete the required number of modules to graduate.

During his time in Canada, Ken had one other thing on his busy mind that wouldn't go away. Before he had left the Tea Estate, his mother wrote to him and suggested that one of the girls from their youth group, Jill Ellis, would make a good wife for him. Ken told his mother that he would find his own wife! But he remembered Jill, and now found thoughts of her invading his mind and he began to wonder whether she really would make a good wife. Was this also God's will for him?

Jill was doing her teacher training at the college which was near Ken's parents' home. Some of the students from the college attended the weekly fellowship meetings in their home. His parents by then were in their early sixties and, though largely retired from the mission field, were still active in Christian ministry in Rwanda. In 1957 when they went to Uganda, where Lawrence was still Archdeacon of Ankole-Kigezi Diocese, Jill lived in their house and continued to look after it and any visitors from Africa who came to stay.

They had both also attended the same church in Penge, where John Collinson was the Vicar. This had given them the opportunity to get to know each other, along with the rest of the youth group. One of the reasons Ken liked Jill was that she stood out from the other girls in the group. They were typically giggly girls that you can find in any group of young people in a church. While she joined in the fun, she had a serious side to her. Her Christian faith was her life and she often expressed it in her willingness to help out whenever she could. She was always keen to attend the fellowship evenings and Bible studies held in the house.

While in Canada, working on the TV's, Ken stayed with his cousin in Toronto. His Canadian wife Graeme was very good at home-making and once again his thoughts turned to Jill and her willing and efficient way of helping out in the home. She would surely make a good wife. Perhaps his mother's advice was not so far from the mark after all!

When he had returned home, in the Easter vacation he asked Jill to play tennis with him. He then asked their vicar, John Collinson, what he would think if he asked Jill to marry him. He knew both of them well and it had been through him that Jill had become the enthusiastic Christian that she was. His answer was emphatic; he said he 'would throw his hat over the house with joy!' Ken then asked this question of his next door neighbour in Herne Hill, Roy Hession (1926-1992), who was a well known conference speaker and author of the famous Christian book, 'The Calvary Road'. This influential book explored the radical Bible teaching on brokenness in the Christian life; a powerful message that sadly, is hardly heard today. Roy Hession had been strongly influenced himself by visits to Rwanda and observing the revival there. They had attended a number of Roy Hession's conferences. He too was very positive about the idea of the marriage. Ken then asked Jill's father who lived in Torquay, who agreed. Jill says that Ken never asked her! She also had one other qualification that was high on the list of Ken's priorities for the ideal wife; she wanted to go to Rwanda as a missionary!

It may seem a little strange to young people of this generation that Christian couples in those days didn't indulge in the same overt courting and romance we are familiar with today. We should remember that this was a different time and generation. These two were serious about their faith and regarded it as inappropriate to behave in any other way. Once they began playing tennis and spending time together, it was an assumption between them that they would marry. In fact, they would not have been together in this innocent way if marriage had not been their aim and desire. Perhaps it is a good example for young people of today to learn about and ponder its merits!

They had a year's engagement, during which Ken completed his first year as a curate at St George's in Worthing. One of the teenagers in their youth group was Garth Hewitt, who later became a well-known Christian musician. Garth trained for the ministry and several years later became Ken's curate. Garth had an unusual appearance for a Church of England curate in that he had long hair.

This had become acceptable for people like the Beatles and the Rolling Stones, but it was very radical for a clergyman!

Ken and Jill were married at St George's church on 25th July 1964. Ken was twenty eight years old. It was a very hot day and the church was packed. Relatives and friends helped to make the service very special. The reception in the church hall was simple and the hall was beautifully decorated by the church ladies. Jill's uncle made the speech representing her father. Jill's father had been strongly opposed to her Christianity. He is not the first father to think that his son or daughter had gone off the rails by becoming what he saw as a fanatical Christian. He may have realised that at the wedding he would be surrounded by Christians of the same ilk and didn't feel he was the right person to give the father-of-the-bride speech. As things turned out, Jill's parents were very impressed with the wedding, the obvious joy of the guests and the general atmosphere.

Jill's uncle was the Lord Mayor of Torquay, well accustomed to public speaking and proposing toasts – usually with fine Champagne. This wedding reception was a non-alcoholic event. He drew a round of laughter at the toast to the Bride when he said 'This is the first time I've given a toast in orange juice!' (In fact it was a fruit cup). A friend loaned them their flat at Versoix, a town on Lake Geneva in Switzerland, for their honeymoon. In later years when God had given them a family, they bought a tent and spent every holiday for many years, camping by that lake at Nyon.

Before the end of their first year in Worthing, their daughter Susan was born. Prior to their marriage, Jill had been accepted by the Ruanda Mission (CMS) as a missionary candidate. Given Ken's background and love of that part of the world, it was only natural that in the back of their minds there was the possibility that God would call them there as a missionary family. The political situation in Africa had changed dramatically as the 'wind of change' was blowing and Kenya (1963), Uganda (1962) and Rwanda (1962) had all gained their independence from colonial rule to become independent states, during the few years that Ken had been back in England. The place for missionaries in these countries was, at that stage, uncertain. Notwithstanding the developments in East Africa, Ken and Jill would not hesitate to go if God called them there as missionaries. As always, they just wanted to be sure that they had heard God's opinion on the matter.

The diocese informed Ken that the allowance available for his position was not enough for a married couple. They gave them two choices, they could try to manage on the single man's allowance or move on to another parish. As they were praying about their situation, Eric McLellan who was Rector of St. Nicholas in Sevenoaks suggested that Ken come to his church for a second curacy while they were seeking God's will on the matter. This was a good suggestion and they decided to accept the position. Sue was still a baby and this gave them time to pray about their next step. The year was 1965, Harold Wilson was Prime Minister, a television licence cost five pounds and very high inflation seemed to do little to dampen 'The swinging sixties'.

They borrowed a coal lorry from their coal man in Worthing, who was a friend, and loaded their belongings on it together with some of the youth group to look after everything. One of the group on the back was Garth Hewitt. His task was holding Ken's African Grey parrot called 'Scruffy', which he had brought with him from Uganda. Ken had acquired the parrot as a 'scruffy little ball of feathers' while working on the farm in Uganda and raised it as a pet.

Scruffy seemed invigorated by the open air journey and talked endlessly, *'I'm Ken Barham's bird.' 'Where's Ken?' or 'Baa baa bla shee have you any wool.'* Ken's brother Ian had tried to teach Scruffy to pronounce his consonants, so he then added *'baa baa k sh have you any wool!'*

One Sunday evening in their house in Sevenoaks, the young people had all gathered as usual for their regular 'Contact' meeting, for which Ken was responsible. They crowded round the parrot trying to persuade him to talk, which he refused to do! The guest speaker, Dr Ken Moynagh, arrived and the young people settled in the lounge. Hush was called for as they began to pray. Not appreciating the quiet, Scruffy, who was stationed in the adjoining hallway, decided to break the silence and started squawking loudly his usual repertoire: *'I'm Ken Barham's bird'* etc.! Prayer was resumed when the unspiritual Scruffy was moved to the other end of the house.

One of the young Christians in the group at that time was a young man called Paul Settatree. Now, more than forty years later, he fondly recalls some of the good experiences he had with the 'Contact' group and in particular, Ken and Jill's formative influence on his life. Paul also recalls, probably because it involved him, that the boys were very interested in the girls and vice versa!

The most obvious characteristic of Ken and Jill that influenced him was their utter sincerity. They inspired Paul to work very hard at his studies and achieve beyond his, or anyone else's expectation. This enabled him to apply and take up a Voluntary Service Overseas (VSO) appointment with the Ruanda Mission. He had no interest in going to university, just a passion to emulate the 'clean, clear, straight-talking, straight-living man of boundless charm and energy' which he had found in Ken.

That determination helped him through many trials that were to come his way in Africa. Through it all, he always remembered the Christian demeanour of Ken and Jill. When, for a season he wandered away from his faith to do his own thing; it was the hard evidence of Ken and Jill's life, along with the example of two or three others that brought him back to a living faith in Christ and a lifelong Christian commitment, along with a love for Africa. To this day he can remember Ken at a house party at Studleigh Court in Devon, thumping the table to keep time and singing with a great radiant smile on his face 'Oh happy day that fixed my choice, on Thee my Saviour and my God.'

Paul also recalls that baby Sue was, of course, a massive attraction to the 'Contact' girls who formed a willing queue of wannabe babysitters. He too, cannot forget Scruffy the parrot curtailing overlong youth prayers with a very timely screech of 'Amen'. Such memories are a precious addition to anyone's portfolio of blessings in the Christian life and their effectiveness in forming Christian character should never be underestimated.

CHAPTER NINE

An Unexpected Change of Direction

During Ken's third year as a curate and his first year at St. Nicholas in Sevenoaks, the couple felt confident enough to apply for missionary training college. This was to be their first step toward serving in Rwanda. No one doubted that Ken and Jill would be welcomed with open arms into the missionary community. They were ideal candidates. Jill was a trained teacher who had already been accepted as a candidate for Rwanda and Ken had been born and raised in that area and was proficient in several of the local languages. Their acceptance was more or less a foregone conclusion; God was surely leading them in this direction. By August 1966 all the required interviews had been completed and the CMS Council had accepted them. They were ready for training and then to uproot and travel to the recently independent Uganda, as a family.

However, not for the first time, Ken found that God's ways are not always our ways. That God's plan is sometimes not what we expect, and in the words of an old saying: ' *We must trust Him where we cannot trace Him.* ' Jill was five months pregnant with their second child when she woke up one morning with a peculiar and worrying sensation in her eyes. Ken called the doctor who examined her and promptly sent her to Sevenoaks Hospital for further investigation. The specialist there sent her to the Nervous Diseases Hospital in Queens Square, London on 27th October 1966. It was one of those situations when Christians find that worry, and trusting in God, are fierce competitors in their minds.

After a week of tests, the specialist, Dr. Gautier-Smith, called Ken to his office and told him that Jill had 'Disseminated Sclerosis', now known as Multiple Sclerosis (MS) for which there was no medical cure. He said they should expect advancing paralysis in her limbs as the nerves were slowly attacked. This seemed to brush aside all their plans and hopes for ministry in Rwanda.

Ken's heart had been filled with visions of what they might be doing in the land that he loved and for the God they both served. It is at times of testing such as this that Christians have to believe and live out some of the hymns and choruses they so easily sing. A popular hymn of that time was particularly relevant to their situation. It has the following lines:

Simply trusting every day;
Trusting through a stormy way;
Even when my faith is small,
Trusting Jesus, that is all.
Trusting as the moments fly,
Trusting as the days go by,
Trusting Him, whate'er befall,
Trusting Jesus, that is all.

The MS didn't prevent the safe birth of their second daughter, Jane. It did however completely change their plans for the future. Dr Adeney, the General Secretary of the Ruanda Mission, informed them that, sadly, they could no longer go to Africa as missionaries. As Ken and Jill peered into an uncertain future, they set themselves to trust God and live one day at a time. They stayed on in Sevenoaks and were wonderfully cared for by the loving church members.

They set up a 'coffee bar' which they called 'The Ark' in a vacant shop in the High Street as part of a Church evangelistic mission to the town. It was so successful that the Church decided to create a more permanent one. They cleared out a cellar under the church hall and, adding suitable décor, called it 'The Cavern'. Ken spent six months running it as well as starting a group for 'older young people'.

In 1967 they moved to a new post for Ken as 'Curate in charge' of St Barnabas, Cheltenham. This was part of a large parish with four churches. Their area was predominantly blocks of council flats; not what comes to mind when one thinks of Cheltenham! Never a person to be content with doing just one thing, Ken was soon involved in the use of a newly built church hall, where they opened another 'coffee bar' and invited local young people to come once a week. The programme was largely pop music, soft drinks and an epilogue to try and reach the 'unclubable' teenagers of the area. Garth Hewitt was among those who came to perform live music.

Although they saw conversions to Christ through this coffee bar, not all church members approved. There was a pub next door and some young people had started coming into the hall in a drunken state. They were using the toilets, being sick in the basins, leaving the taps running, removing the toilet chains, and generally leaving a terrible mess. Many hours were spent clearing up after closing time. There were negative comments from some older church members, such as, 'You are spoiling our new hall.' But Ken felt the Church was making some headway in the council flats so it was worth the effort.

One day they received a phone call from Ken's mother saying his father had been taken to St George's Hospital with a second heart attack. They raced from Cheltenham to London and found Ken's father in the intensive care ward with doctors applying shock treatment to his heart. Ken's mother was outside watching as the heart failed to start pumping. In a moment of either inspiration or desperation, or both, she pushed her way into the room and took his hand and said *'Lawrence.'* His heart started immediately! When Ken and Jill arrived and were ushered in, Ken's father said, *'That was a near one!'*

Their two girls, Sue and Jane, were now four and two years old. Ken and Jill constantly remembered the words of the consultant in Queens Square; the prognosis for her disease was daunting. They hoped and prayed for the best, but inwardly prepared themselves for the possibility of the opposite. One Sunday morning Jill woke up early with no feeling in her legs. Ken made her a cup of tea and came back to pray with her. As he knelt at her bedside he looked at a Bible text they had been given in Sevenoaks which hung over the bed. It read *'Trust in the Lord. He faileth not and forsaketh not His saints.'* As they prayed, this text was speaking to them. God does not make a mistake, of this Ken was sure. They were His and He loved them; they were to trust Him. Ken's heart cried out to God, 'But Lord what about Jill's legs?' 'How can I run a church, look after two children and a disabled wife?'

The Lord helped them through; He brought them to a place in their hearts where they could genuinely say 'Your will be done. Lord we know you can heal, but if your will is for me to look after the family, then please enable me.' This was a very big crisis which they now faced. The reality of what MS can do now loomed menacingly before them. It was a Sunday morning and a busy day lay ahead. Ken phoned his mother and the Vicar of St. Marks to ask them to pray. He then dressed Jill and the children, loaded them into the car and drove to St Barnabas.

He took the children to the Sunday school, helped Jill

to a seat at the back of the church and went to the pulpit. Ken was sharing with the congregation their early morning experience and how they came to trust the Lord, when Jill motioned from the back that the feeling in her legs had come back! Events like that bring you closer to your congregation and there was a great feeling of joy as they abandoned the normal liturgy and joined in spontaneous prayer and praise.

Ken and Jill were filled with joy because it was obvious that God had done a work of healing; Jill was walking around as living proof. Was this a permanent healing? Would any other MS symptoms occur? Was this just an unusual remission in the MS itself? There was one thing that didn't change; they still had to trust God and live one day at a time.

About a year after this healing experience they went to see their friend, Dr Doug Calcott; who now lived in Worcester. This was the same Dr Doug Calcott who had trusted Ken with his big Ford car when he was just seventeen and who helped to run the Crusader class in Nairobi. He was an eye surgeon and when he examined Jill's eyes, he could find no damage to the optic nerve. He also sent them to see a man who used sound waves to deal with her frozen arm. The man was a bit 'different' being alternative in both practice and appearance, but they trusted Doug Calcott's recommendation. Jill went weekly for this treatment and each week an envelope was pushed under their door to cover the cost. They were grateful to their mystery donor and to God for this provision. (Because the cost of the treatment was stretching their finances) No one becomes a clergyman in the Church of England because it is well paid!

They wanted to add to their family, but had been told that MS is exacerbated by childbirth. They consulted Dr.

Calcott and he said that he could see no remaining symptoms or any reason why they shouldn't go ahead and have another baby. Michael was born in Maidstone in 1971; his birth was easy and Jill's health improved dramatically. To this day, Jill has had no further symptoms of MS. God had done one of His miracles and the healing of Jill's MS was instant, complete, permanent and medically inexplicable.

*　　*　　*

First living

This Anglican term simply means being appointed to the post of a Vicar or Rector, responsible for a whole parish. After three years in Cheltenham Ken was offered the 'Living' of St Luke's, Maidstone. In April 1970 they moved from the Curate's bungalow to a large seven bedroom Victorian vicarage in a growing parish of ten thousand in Maidstone. It was a 'Training Parish' which was allocated two full time assistant curates, who normally served for three years before moving on to a more senior post or a Living of their own.

He inherited a curate, David Williams, and a parish worker, Josie Midwinter. David was a highly organised person who worked on his sermon at the beginning of the week and put it in the file until Sunday; unlike Ken whose busy schedule usually resulted in a Saturday slog! Garth Hewitt, whose father had been Ken's first vicar, was now a curate himself and was Ken's first chosen curate.

Garth was already making a name for himself as a gospel singer. He played guitar and mouth organ and wrote his own lyrics. His music and trendy long hair attracted the attention of the local media who were very interested in this Rock n' Roll curate. Ken was perhaps more open minded than some of his more traditionalist colleagues might have been and encouraged Garth in this aspect of his ministry. He soon went on to record his first album *'The lion and the lamb'*. The church needed to pray hard for him on that occasion because his throat was rough when he went to the studio, but the recording went well.

Garth's songs have inspired many people to look at the suffering of places like Uganda in the post Idi Amin years, Bangladesh, South Africa and other troubled places in the world. Garth's work included 'Justice in Palestine'. There is no doubt that Ken's influence fired him up to some degree by his obvious love for Africa and the many stories from East Africa, expressed so often in the Vicarage. It was obvious to anyone who knew Ken that he had left more than his belongings at the tea plantation; part of his heart was still in Africa. Ken and Jill had no idea why God had not allowed them to pursue their original plan. It would be many years later, and with the benefit of hindsight, that they could look back and have the satisfaction of observing the confirmation of the truth that they had clung to; *God does not make mistakes!*

For a year they had a Ugandan cleric called Abraham Zaribugire as a third curate. Ken sent him visiting in the new housing development where young couples were buying their first homes. This would appear to be a daunting task for an African who spoke with an accent that hearers just couldn't place. Nevertheless, Abraham's broad African smile and his dog collar combined to break down any initial suspicion. His formula was brilliant, if unconventional. He knocked on the door and informed the baffled occupant that the vicar had sent him to visit them. Once seated in the home and with introductions completed, he would ask the couple if they had a Bible in the house. Generally they could find one somewhere. Then he told them he was not good at reading English and could they help him by finding and reading John 3:16 or some similar passage. He thanked them for their help and proceeded to give them his testimony, followed by an invitation to take advantage of any of the church's activities or services. As young couples starting families, many were interested in the baptisms that usually took place on Sunday afternoons followed by tea at the vicarage and an invitation to any of the church's activities or services. Ken soon discovered that they were virtually building their congregation from the visits by Abraham before and after the baptisms.

Abraham was with them over one winter when it snowed heavily. He had never seen snow and was as excited as the children. He even filled a bottle with snow hoping to take it back to Uganda to show his wife! He had great fun pulling the children round and round the garden on their sledge.

One Sunday at St. Luke's, Ken had prepared five year old twins for baptism. On the morning of the baptism his brother, who was also a clergyman, phoned urgently from Suffolk and asked Ken for help. The situation must have been serious because Ken asked the then curate, Chris Grundy, to deputise for him and conduct the baptism service. Chris had no children and was quite unused to handling them, but bravely said he would. This allowed Ken to respond to the urgent call and he immediately drove to Suffolk.

On his return he asked Chris how it had gone. He replied, *'One got away!'* Ken went to see the parents who told the whole story. Inexperienced as Chris was, he had picked up one of the five year old, red headed twins in his arms as you would a baby, ready to baptize her. The other twin, not liking what she saw one little bit, ran off and headed for home! Ken fixed a new date and the mum agreed, 'as long as it was not that young man!' Later, Chris was married to a lovely girl Anne, who was an Occupational Therapist. Ken and Jill's daughter Sue was so impressed with Anne that she decided on an OT career for herself – and that is exactly what she did. The Barham family had almost ten happy years in that big Victorian vicarage and they all loved it. It was an ideal house with lots of space for their growing children.

Shortly after his appointment to St Luke's, Ken discovered that the church had a long-standing project to build a church hall which had been planned since before the Second World War! Their initial funds were used up in the war effort. In the 1960's they had had an architect's estimate for £4,000, but had failed to grasp the nettle and again the plan stalled. Ken decided that something should be done to make the plan a reality. A church hall would be very useful. The project was discussed with the Church Council and it was agreed that they should arrange to have a new plan drawn up. This involved removing the narthex (the church entrance lobby) and creating a vestibule connecting the nineteenth century church and the proposed new hall. Similar improvements have been carried out in many traditional church buildings in the UK. The estimate was £30,000, which was considered a very large amount in 1971. They took a vote at the Church Council and it was passed by a large majority. The Treasurer and a Church Warden voted against it. An unavoidable consequence of most such votes is that the result often produces a disgruntled minority.

A few weeks later Ken was called by the Archdeacon in Canterbury, who asked if he would visit him to talk about the project and he agreed. The Church Warden had written to the Archdeacon saying 'The Vicar has made a big mistake in embarking on a project which this parish has no chance of funding!' When Ken arrived in Canterbury he was invited into the office of the Diocesan Secretary. He informed Ken about the Church Warden's letter and asked how he proposed to find £30,000. Not intimidated, Ken told him that his understanding of working for God was that you first discover if the matter was in the will of God. If it was, then the Lord would provide. God uses people and therefore they must work hard and pray hard. Taking this spiritual high ground may silence the likes of doubting Diocesan Secretaries and Church Wardens, but now Ken had to 'put his faith where his mouth was'.

Up to this point, Ken, with some members of the church, had met at 7.00 a.m. each Saturday morning to pray. Now it was time to put legs on their prayers. One lady made fudge and sold it, another retailed eggs, they all collected newspapers and stored them in the Vicarage cellar until collection, and everyone committed themselves to give what they could. To Ken's amazement, the Diocesan Secretary, Mr. Carlisle, told him that they had an unusual connection. He had been the government officer in Tanzania who brought his wife to their mission hospital in Burundi to be delivered of their baby. Furthermore, he had purchased their black Ford Consul which Ken had carefully cleaned and polished inside and out! The matter was concluded when the Diocese gave their blessing and guaranteed a bank loan for the remainder of the money. The hall project succeeded.

CHAPTER TEN

A New Door Opens

While working as the Vicar of St. Luke's in Maidstone, Ken was asked to serve as a member of the council of the Ruanda Mission (CMS). He was happy to accept the invitation because it helped him to keep in touch with Rwanda. Then in 1979 the Mission agreed to appoint a full time Travelling Secretary for England, based in the Midlands. To fill this role the Council proposed bringing home an experienced missionary for the job. Ken, however, felt this was wasteful of a precious resource for an experienced couple who had learnt the local language and were well integrated into the Church work.

As so often happens when someone says something like that, the Council said 'If you think that's a bad idea would you consider doing it yourself?'

This was not an easy decision because Jill had a teaching job in Detling, which she enjoyed, especially as she had built up a rapport with the gypsy families in 'Plumtree Bottom'. This was a local valley where a group of notorious gypsies had established a semi-permanent caravan site, much to the annoyance of the local residents. They were accused of stealing cars and other anti-social behaviour. Unlike others in the area, Ken and Jill went out of their way to show Christian love and friendship to these families. The children continued in school largely because of Jill's efforts to interest them in their education. They made cakes in her class for their own parents' evenings and often brought in trays of strawberries and cherries. Ken baptised some of the children and gave them tea in the vicarage garden as was his custom. It is never easy to walk away from relationships such as these, but they knew in their hearts that they were following God's leading and the consequences could be safely left in His hands.

Jill's salary just covered the school fees of Sue and Jane at Wadhurst College. They wanted to be sure that this was God's plan for them, so they 'put out a fleece'. This Old Testament reference (Judges 6:37) refers to a means of finding assurance from God that they were following His will by asking God for a sign. Ken asked the Council if they would agree to divide England into two areas. As a travelling secretary he would cover the area from Derby to Land's End, and someone else would cover the area north of that. As there was no house available with this role, he also requested that the family move to their bungalow in Battle, which they had bought for their retirement in twenty seven years time.

If the Mission agreed to these two requests they would accept the offer of the job and trust that Jill would find a teaching post in the Battle area. The Mission did agree and they took this as the sign they needed. Ken resigned from his post at St. Luke's and the family had to make preparations to leave the vicarage and squeeze into the bungalow, which is called 'Rosewood'. Later they added two extra bedrooms and a double garage to ease their crowded situation. Ken, ever the practical man, did most of the work himself. The bungalow is in a pleasant rural setting surrounded by fields, but within easy reach of the town of Battle. They have lived in Rosewood, with their dogs, ever since.

With Jill teaching and the two girls away at school, building the extensions at Rosewood was a task undertaken on Ken's days off. The routine was for Ken and Michael, now aged three, to take the number five bus from Maidstone to Battle, mix the cement, lay a few rows of bricks, cut the grass and return home. The work was also a healthy diversion from normal parish work and served as an outlet for Ken's creativity and his love of building. The urge to build was God-given in Ken and a gift that always proved useful in much of Ken's life and ministry in Africa.

After sending the relevant card to the Building Inspector asking him to come and check the trench for the foundations, the day for inspection arrived. At various stages of any building work, even extensions, inspectors are required to check that everything is done according to the national building specifications before the work can continue. The first inspection is usually to check that the trench for the foundations is deep enough. Ken and his son Michael were already on site, having travelled by bus, when the inspector from the council department arrived. Michael was down in the metre deep trench with his bucket and spade clearing out the loose soil that had fallen in since the

Repairing the chimney

previous week. He might have been very young, but he took his work seriously. The Inspector came, looked at his notes and saw the name of the builder; 'Barham and Son'. He looked at Michael, whose head barely reached ground level, and asked if he was the 'Son'. Ken informed him that Michael was indeed the 'Son'. The inspector laughed and laughed. This first contact with the inspector developed into a very useful friendship. Michael on the other hand, must have wondered what was so funny about the important work he was doing for Daddy.

*   *   *

Returning to Rwanda

As Ken had hoped, his work as a travelling secretary for the Ruanda Mission now required him to travel to their mission field to meet the mission's workers and see their work; the prospect was exciting. What changes would he find after so long? How well would he remember the languages? His mind buzzed with questions and anticipation.

So in October 1979 Ken, now aged forty three, returned to Rwanda and Burundi for the first time in twenty-four years. The visit was sponsored by the mission and Ken was accompanied by Ossie Post, who had been recruited by the mission to represent them in the north of England as Ken had for the south. The purpose of a travelling secretary is to promote and inform people, mainly in churches, about the work of the mission. Hopefully this would motivate them to pray for the work and support it financially.

Representing any mission is more authentic and powerful if the speaker has actually been to see the location of the mission's work. If the worker can say to a congregation: 'I have seen this myself... I have spoken to this or that missionary about this and they told me... I have taken these photos or slides myself when I was visiting…etc, it carries more weight. For both Ken and his colleague Ossie, their visit was going to add an important dimension to their work and its effectiveness.

Their route took them via Heathrow, Brussels, Nairobi and Kigali, with the then national airline of Belgium, Sabena. When Ken left Rwanda for the UK in 1955, Kigali was a small town dwarfed by Butare. Now he could see that there had been huge developments in Kigali during the sixties and the road from Kigali to Butare (80 miles), which had been a mud road, was being surfaced with tarmac for the first time, by a French company. There were new multi-story buildings and shops in town, most of which had been established since independence in 1962. Travelling with different missionaries they were able to visit mission centres in south-west Uganda, Rwanda and Burundi.

While in Butare they visited Justin Ndandali, the Archbishop of the Province of Burundi, Rwanda and Zaire. Ken already knew Justin because while he was studying in Bristol he had spent his holidays at Ken's parents' home in London and at Ken's home in Sevenoaks.

At this point, another important development in Ken's ministry presented itself. The Archbishop made an unusual request; he wanted Ken to return regularly to Rwanda and help him by providing in-service training for his clergy in their parishes. Ken's immediate response was positive. He would need to consult with people he was working for in the UK, but the prospect was exciting.

*   *   *

A family adventure

Ken's next trip to Rwanda was in 1981 and would prove to be very different indeed. He decided to take the family with him. He and Jill now had three children: Sue was sixteen,

Jane fourteen and Michael (the Master Builder) was now ten. None of Ken's family had ever been to Africa and he naturally wanted them to see the country where he had grown up, to appreciate why he loved the place, and hopefully share his enthusiasm and vision for it. A kind friend helped with the airfares, making the trip possible and they set out on their great family adventure.

Ken's family could be excused if they had built up in their minds an idealised vision of what East Africa was like. They had heard stories of Ken's happy life there and imagined what a wonderful part of the world it was. They were however, in for a shock! Reality awaited them on a narrow finger of land reaching out from the northern shores of Lake Victoria and only a couple of miles north of the Equator – at Entebbe International Airport.

They landed at Entebbe, Uganda's main airport, on an Air France flight and walked from the aircraft through an avenue of Ugandan soldiers. The soldiers seemed tense and wary. The atmosphere was menacing in the way it can be when young men with guns are watching you with suspicion in their eyes. One can only pray and hope that they are not drunk. This was not the welcome to Africa that Ken would have chosen for his family's first trip!

The whole country was tense. Apart from the fact that the President, Milton Obote was only in the second year of his brutal and oppressive second spell of ruling Uganda, a bush war to oust him was just commencing. The insurgents were invading from Tanzania and were being led by Paulo Muwanga, whose deputy was Yoweri Museveni, who would eventually become President of Uganda in 1986.

Amazingly, Entebbe airport was still in a terrible mess five years after the 'Entebbe Raid' of 4th July 1976 when Idi Amin (deposed on 11 April 1979) had held hostage an Air

France 747 aircraft travelling from Israel. The aircraft had been highjacked by Palestinian terrorists and ordered to land at Entebbe. Non-Jewish passengers were released but the one hundred and four Jewish passengers were removed from the aircraft and detained in the airport terminal. All but one of the hostages (she was murdered in hospital) were dramatically rescued by an Israeli Special Forces unit comprising one hundred elite Commandos. The hospital patient murdered was Dora Bloch, a 75-year-old British Jewish immigrant, who was taken to Mulago Hospital in Kampala and murdered by Ugandan officials on the orders of Idi Amin. Some of her doctors and nurses were also murdered for apparently trying to intervene. The rescue was codenamed 'Operation Thunderbolt'. The airport was still chaotic with not a single item of furniture and had countless bullet holes in the walls of the buildings from the raid.

Before their departure, Ken had written to Kabale Prep School, where he had started his schooling aged five, and asked them if there was anything that they could bring them from the UK. Their reply was a challenge; they wanted washing machines! Obviously, washing machines are not normal luggage, they were large and heavy. Nevertheless, Ken's can-do approach to life ensured that they bought two twin tubs, and as a bonus packed them with much needed medicines, which were donated by various chemists. There were a variety of medicines and Ken had listed them for the benefit of the customs officials.

When they collected their luggage at Entebbe Airport, including the two washing machines, they headed for the door. There was no desk or barrier and the whole building seemed full of soldiers and passengers. They were stopped by a man who they presumed was a customs official. One or two of their suitcases were emptied on the floor for inspection. The man then asked what was in the two big boxes. Ken said they were full of medicines, hoping this would be sufficient explanation. He asked what sort of medicines. Ken produced his list. He then wanted to look at them, so Ken opened the top and revealed dozens of bottles and packets. He looked at the list and asked which was which, to which Ken replied that he was not a doctor and wouldn't have a clue which bottle applied to which name on the list. Ken offered to let him keep the list but he told Ken that he would need it at the road blocks. Seeing the rest of the luggage and the three rather nervous children, he finally said they could go. In retrospect Ken realized that he had forgotten to tell him that the boxes were in fact washing machines!

One has to have been in a similar situation to this one, with the uneasy atmosphere, uncertainty, natural fear, and parental concern for the children, to fully appreciate the immense relief that Ken and Jill must have felt when they were told they could go. It is impossible for us to guess what went on in the mind of this isolated customs official; if that is what he was? Perhaps, like many Africans, he still had a respect for the clergy? Perhaps he was thrown off balance by the arrival of such an unusual group at that time, with their amazing luggage? Add to this that Ken was able to address him in Swahili, the Lingua franca of East Africa, could only add to the man's uncertainty.

Ken soon noticed that many of the shops in Uganda were boarded up. They had been owned by the Asians whom Idi Amin had driven out of the country in 1972. He had given the 80,000 ethnic Indians ninety days to leave the country. Fifty thousand of them had British passports and many came to Britain. Most of these families had originally been brought to Uganda by the British, some up to a hundred years before as part of the colonial development. As in many African countries, the Asian population were the backbone of the retail and business communities. Their departure caused the economic situation in Uganda to deteriorate even further, and was one of the most inept actions of Idi Amin's chaotic, corrupt and brutal administration.

They stayed initially with Dr Davies at Mengo Hospital in Kampala before heading south west to Kisiizi. Mengo hospital was the first hospital in East Africa, built in 1897 by Sir Albert Cook (1870-1951) and it is still operating today. It was originally owned by the Church Missionary Society, but in 1958 the hospital was handed over by the CMS to an independent and autonomous Board of Governors and Registered Trustees.

The family and their excess luggage were met at the airport by an ambulance and a pick-up. The ambulance was from Kisiizi, which was their next destination. It had travelled the three hundred miles to Kampala to collect supplies and deliver patients to Mengo Hospital. It even looked like an ambulance; it was painted yellow, had a flashing blue light on top and Kisiizi Hospital emblazoned on the side. They piled their luggage and the two machines into the ambulance and the pickup and set off for Kampala. The road into the capital had numerous road blocks, making the one-hour journey much slower and further contributed to the atmosphere of tension.

In most parts of Africa, road blocks are part of the scenery and often have to be negotiated with caution and a show of respect. There are two main types: one is manned by police, the other by soldiers – occasionally by both. Police are more likely to want a bribe whereas soldiers are more likely to do their job properly. The road blocks on their journey into Kampala were manned by soldiers. You just hope they are not drunk, which occasionally is the case. It is advisable to come to a halt slowly, have your window already down and your sun glasses removed. Then greet the man with a smile and ask 'How are you today?'

Ken was in the front passenger seat in the pick-up and had one important advantage; he was able to talk his way through the road blocks in Luganda, the local language. The family were behind in the ambulance and were often delayed by the soldiers who asked lots of questions. Ken frequently had to get out and go back to rescue them. After what seemed like ages, all the road blocks on the twenty one mile journey to Kampala were successfully negotiated.

They were taken to the home of Dr. Davies and his wife who were missionaries with the Ruanda Mission. Here they were made welcome and were able to relax a little. Everyone breathed a big sigh of relief and felt thankful to God for their safe arrival. That evening there was a mighty tropical storm and everyone had to find some receptacle that would hold water and put it outside to collect the rain water to augment the very meagre water supply. Presidents Idi Amin and Milton Obote between them had totally ruined Uganda and every part of the infrastructure was in tatters. Driving through Kampala city next day was difficult, every road being just a collection of potholes. There were mountains of rubbish scattered all over the streets to add to the atmosphere of neglect and desolation.

Jill remembers the curfew and the many dogs barking in the night, which, added to the sporadic gunshots, made it difficult to sleep. Every African town has a canine sub-culture which comes alive at night, determined to communicate with every other dog within barking, yapping or howling range; but the addition of gunfire maintained the same insecure atmosphere as the daytime. We can appreciate that Ken had some idea of what the family was going to see in Africa, but the menacing atmosphere and the tension that they experienced in Uganda was perhaps unexpected. Jill needed immense courage as a mother trying to allay the natural fears for her children. Whatever fear she felt, she needed to put on a brave face to reduce any alarm the children felt, especially the teenage girls. It is true that God was watching over them, but on a purely human level, this was a dangerous and unpredictable environment.

This was the family's baptism into Africa and they must have wondered just what Dad had got them into! It certainly wasn't a water baptism because there was no water. This was indicative of the level of government incompetence in a land with a plentiful rainfall and known as 'The Pearl of Africa'. A mug full of water had to suffice for washing, brushing their teeth and then the remains used to tip into the cistern for the inside toilet! This toilet was to be used only in an emergency at night. During the day they had to use a 'long drop' pit latrine down in the garden which had no door catch and was shared with the house next door! Someone had to stand guard for another member of the family to use it. It is sometimes joked that the only thing worse than a 'long drop' is a 'short drop'! This very English family were not thrilled about this. No description of an African pit latrine could do justice to the actual experience of using one!

Michael, now aged ten, was totally unable to eat the dry food and was greatly relieved when it was time for their journey in the hospital ambulance to Dr Bill Cave's house at Kisiizi, three hundred miles south. Bill, with his family, worked there with the Ruanda Mission. Needless to say, the road was in an appalling condition. With so many potholes in the tarmac it was easier to drive on the dirt tracks at the side of the road; a choice made by most of the vehicles on this route.

It would be reasonable to expect that, after the traumas of their first visit, Ken and Jill's three children would not want to visit this area ever again or perhaps even step foot outside the UK. In fact, they have all been to Rwanda several times since then. Sue worked at Gahini Hospital in Eastern Rwanda as an Occupational Therapist for six months after her graduation. Now, Sue and her husband are missionaries with the Latin American Mission in Honduras.They have three children Joshua, Hannah and Theo. Jane was stationed in Cyangugu, Rwanda in 1994, working with the International Rescue Committee, having been withdrawn from Somalia. She has since worked for many NGOs and the UN in Iraq, Turkey, Djibouti, Zaire, Tanzania, Zambia, then with her husband in Sudan and Sri Lanka, and more recently, Pakistan, and Borneo. Wherever there are disasters, she is likely to be sent there. In recognition of her outstanding work, she was awarded the **OBE** in the 2011 Queen's Birthday Honours for 'Humanitarian Aid Advisor.for services to humanitarian aid in Sri Lanka'. Her husband Alistair with Alannah and Maisie will accompany her to the Palace.

Michael has been to Rwanda five times on different assignments. He spent three months working with Michael Greig on tree planting, living alone in Ken's house at Butare. Later, he spent some weeks there with a mechanic friend putting a new chassis on one of Ken's Land Rovers. He also spent some time at Peace Guest House, Cyangugu teaching a team of local volunteers to build the first of the five rondavels (round African houses) as part of the development programme there. He now lives in New Zealand with his wife Debbie and children Gemma and Danny.

Michael, thirty years later, has some interesting insights into his own experience, not just of that first trip to Africa, but the trips he has made as an adult. Memories of his first trip on 1981 are typical of a ten-year-old-boy – dominated by the diet. The matoke in Kampala, dry sorghum porridge in Kabale, and stewed goat in a rural parish, all gave him a new-found respect for his mother's cooking – at least she removed the hooves before the meat went in the pot!

Michael attributes his experiences in Africa with providing opportunities to gain insight into more than just another culture and country, but into his father too. It was in subsequent visits that Michael came to realise the impact that Africa had on his father. Most people who go to Africa to work – even for a short time – will later testify that Africa changed them more than they changed Africa. Michael observed that his father excelled in areas of gifting and endurance not normally required back home in England. Africa had given him an ability to withstand difficult and uncomfortable circumstances. A hand of bananas and a tin of cold baked beans was enough to sustain his Dad for a whole day's work – a day that might see a continual stream of people at his door from 5am to 11 pm, or might include a poor widow requesting a pig for income to support her family.

Michael fondly remembers seeing a lighter side to his father in Africa too. Imagine the waiter's embarrassment after making comments to his colleagues as this quintessential English father and son dined, only to have Ken reveal at the end of the meal that he had understood every word, by answering him in his native tongue. Or the momentary panic Michael's cousin must have felt upon discovering Uncle Ken had been offered a number of cows for her hand in marriage! In getting to know his father better, Michael feels he has a lot for which to thank Africa.

Ken and Jill with their children and grandchildren

CHAPTER ELEVEN

A Home From Home

In response to the request from Archbishop Justin Ndandali, from 1981 Ken began visiting parishes in Rwanda, Burundi and Uganda to give the local clergy some in-service training. By accepting this opportunity, Ken was now commencing a whole new dimension to his ministry; one that was going to set the course for much of the rest of his life.

The visits usually lasted a month and Ken would make two visits each year. Initially the task was to get to know the pastors and establish a good relationship of friendship and trust with them. In this, again he had the great advantage of knowing the language and culture of the men he was dealing with. For Ken it was as if he had returned to his own country after a very long vacation; he was, in a special way, 'at home' in the work he was now doing.

He visited rural parishes where he would usually stay in the pastor's house for the night. This enabled him to have meetings with the pastor's family and church leaders. For Ken to sleep in the simple houses of the clergy, eat their food and drink their tea, was not something that most foreign visitors would do. It gave him a credibility and identification with his hosts that added extra power to the ministry of training and encouragement that he was bringing. The Ruanda Mission asked if he could include other areas of their work. This extended his ministry to Kabale, Kisoro in Uganda plus Buye, Matana and Gitega in Burundi.

Justin Ndandali was the Bishop of Butare at that time as well as the Archbishop of the Francophone Province. Justin and his diocesan staff said they would like Ken to be included in their staff and suggested appointing him a Canon of Butare Cathedral. On 30th January 1983 Ken knelt before the Bishop in the cathedral and made the required promises. The Bishop laid his hands on him and commissioned him to assist in the work of the Diocese; a ministry which he continued for the next ten years. This gave Ken authority to speak about the Butare Diocese when seeking funds for the projects, as he was an honorary member of the Cathedral Chapter. Through the visits he gathered knowledge, experience and adventures to share with the congregations and various other groups back home.

With the family now living in Rosewood in Battle, they attended the parish churches of Ashburnham and Penhurst. He had been friends for some time with Revd. John Bickersteth the Vicar. Ken was also able to assist John by helping with the extra work of services at Christmas and Easter. It was a friendship that led to an important change of direction in both their lives, and showed yet again, that God was orchestrating His plan for them both.

While still a student at Oak Hill Theological College, John Bickersteth inherited the Ashburnham estate. On completing his training, he was appointed to this parish because he also needed to oversee the management of the huge estate with its mansion, farms and houses. He ministered in the Parish for twenty six years, during which time he also developed Ashburnham Place as a spiritual retreat and conference centre.

The first records of Ashburnham Place date back to the twelfth century. It was the ancestral seat of the Earls of Ashburnham and in its heyday, one of the finest country houses in England, with its gardens laid out by Capability Brown. The Earldom became extinct on the death of Thomas

Ashburnham, the sixth Earl in 1924. The estate was inherited by his niece Lady Catherine Ashburnham. Lady Catherine was the last of this line of the Ashburnham family, so the estate was inherited by John Bickersteth, the nearest male relative, on her death in 1953. In addition to the prospect of huge repair bills, he was also saddled with crippling death duties. The contents of the house were sold at auction in June and July 1953, and half of the estate itself was sold in the next few years. The house was partly demolished in 1959, reducing the central section to two floors and the wings to a single story. Meanwhile, John Bickersteth established a prayer centre in the stable block. He gave the remaining parts of the house and 220 acres of parkland to the Ashburnham Christian Trust in April 1960. It is now operated as a Christian conference and prayer centre (see www.ashburnham.org.uk). Ashburnham Place now accommodates up to three hundred guests and is constantly being modernised. By 1984 the demands of the different roles had become far too much for one person to manage and John, now aged fifty eight decided it was time to retire from his parish work.

In the Anglican system, each parish has 'Patrons' who have the responsibility to appoint Clergy when vacancies arise. In Ashburnham the Patrons were also the Trustees of the Ashburnham Place Conference Centre. John arranged a meeting with the Trustees/Patrons and suggested that he should retire from parish work to meet the growing demands of the Conference Centre ministry. He suggested that a good replacement for him would be Ken. Paul Broomhall, who was Churchwarden of Penhurst agreed with the idea. Thus it was that Ken was interviewed, accepted, and appointed as the new Vicar of Ashburnham and Penhurst parishes and John officially retired from the post.

Then, to complete a perfect arrangement, the Diocese of Chichester and the Trustees of the two parishes agreed that Ken should continue with the work in Rwanda, visiting as usual for a month, twice a year. To make that possible the Bishop of Lewes (Area Bishop of the Diocese of Chichester which is eighty miles long and has three areas) licensed John Bickersteth as Ken's Assistant Curate. This was perfect team work as John simply took over the services for the month whenever Ken was in Rwanda. The arrangement was very unusual and probably unique.

At the same time, Ken resigned as travelling secretary of the Ruanda Mission. The parish was a small one and although a stipend was provided, the Vicarage had been sold many years earlier. John Bickersteth had not needed accommodation because he lived on the Ashburnham estate. Ken and family were living in Rosewood, so the arrangement was convenient for all concerned, including the diocese.

John also agreed to become Chairman of the Lawrence Barham Memorial Trust. The Mission saw the strategic value of Ken's trips to Rwanda and agreed to fund them; an arrangement that continued until 1991. With the support of the Bishop and the Diocese of Chichester, Ken's work in Africa and the twice yearly ministry visits he made could continue. John's new position as curate meant that Ken didn't have to worry about the parish work while he was away. It was the perfect solution to enable both of these multi-tasking men of God to continue and develop the ministries to which God had called them.

Having run his race in fine form, lived a busy and fruitful life in God's service, John Bickersteth died from cancer in 1991 aged sixty five and went to his reward in heaven. Ken describes his friend as a wise, intellectual and humble man.

The partnership that had been established between Ken and John Bickersteth had lasted six years. Ken's trips to Africa needed to continue, so he had to find Clergy for the two country parishes and services at St Peters, Ashburnham and St Michael in Penhurst when he was away. The solution was a succession of honorary curates, Jim Rex, Len Crowe and Nigel Holmes, who stepped into the breach. In this particular corner of the Anglican world, no one could ever accuse the church of inflexibility!

Ken's programme of fundraising included establishing a registered charity in his father's memory, the 'Lawrence Barham Memorial Trust'. The trust became a vital tool for the extensive fundraising that would be needed for the Rwandan ministry in future years. In most of Africa the two greatest needs of the churches are for good Biblical teaching and the construction of church buildings. African churches will meet under a shady tree if they need to, but with growing numbers the tree would not accommodate them all and in the heavy rains would not keep them dry, so a brick building with an iron roof would be essential to see effective growth of that church, provided the pastor was well trained and diligent in his work. A pastor's house was essential, followed in time by a church school and in some cases a clinic. Thus it was natural that Ken's work took in the twin essentials of developing the man and equipping him with the practical means to work effectively.

This required funds that the African church simply did not have. Now it was becoming clear why God had arranged Ken and Jill's circumstances in such a way, that Ken could train men in Rwanda and raise funds back in the west to aid their ministry. Only God Himself could have envisaged such a unique plan. From Ken and Jill, it required obedience and commitment to fulfil their part of the partnership. The Bible teaches that God stores up the prayers of His people. Perhaps the prayers of all those involved in the revival into which Ken had been born and raised, were still being answered.

*   *   *

Whenever Ken arrived in Africa for one of his ministry trips, his usual pattern was to travel locally in a Land Rover that he had shipped out from the UK. It was equipped with poles carried on the roof rack to help negotiate small broken bridges over streams. He also carried a camp bed and mosquito net. Travel in Africa is rarely straightforward even today. Ken often encountered difficulties from poor roads, heavy rains and mechanical problems with his vehicles. Driving over mountains on rough muddy roads would be considered a dangerous occupation for most Westerners visiting this region; for Ken it was difficult, but second nature. Living and working in Africa had equipped him more than most for the difficult driving conditions.

On one such visit, he drove with a pastor to a village called Mpinga, where they wanted to build a church. Changing gear to climb up the steep hill to the site, the gearstick refused to move. He tried everything he could think of, but it wouldn't budge. It was getting late and there was no time to find alternative transport or mechanical help with the Land Rover. There was no alternative but to take out the camp bed and sleeping bag, rig up a pole to hang the mosquito net on and settle down for the night in the open air. The pastor, his son and another man slept in the Land Rover while Ken drifted into a sound sleep to the gentle sounds of the African night.

He was woken by light rain on his face at five o'clock in the morning feeling very refreshed and ready to face whatever the day had for them. At dawn one of the men set off to look for a mechanic at a local rice factory. He soon found one and returned with him on the back of a bicycle. The mechanic managed to dismantle the gear stick and found a way to get into first gear. They drove slowly down the track to the factory where the mechanic worked and he eventually managed to get them back on the road again. In those days – before the great invasion of Japanese 4 x 4 vehicles – anyone in Africa who called himself a mechanic was expected to know how to fix Land Rovers.

The Chinese had begun constructing a much-needed road from the southern town of Butare through the forest to Cyangugu. The excavations to the mud road meant that Ken had to fight his way through the deep mud churned up by their big bulldozers. This was all in a day's work for Ken and his trusty Land Rover.

A further illustration of the dangers of travelling in this particular part of Africa was dramatically illustrated in January 1987. It was an incident that no one would ever describe as 'all in a day's work'! Ken was visiting Banda, a new parish on the edge of the natural forest of Nyungwe. He was travelling with two people from England who were on their first visit to Africa, John French aged twenty nine and a courageous septuagenarian, Eila McDermot. John had been struggling with a number of difficulties and disappointments in his life and just wanted a new start as a Christian. Eila, aged seventy three, had heard Ken talk a lot about Rwanda and was very interested as her brother had previously worked in Africa. They had had good meetings on the Sunday and settled down for the night in a small mud church. Throughout the night heavy rain fell continuously. In the morning they packed up their sleeping bags and loaded up the Land Rover with their jerry-cans, spare wheels, camp beds and personal supplies. Ken set off down the small dirt track that had been cut into the hillside to form the crude road. He had six passengers, which included the pastor Venuste Mutiganda, his Catechist, and, as so often happens in Africa, a couple of people just wanting a lift. Among these was a lady with a small baby on her lap.

This would be a tricky drive at any time with the Land Rover fully loaded. The heavy rain had turned a difficult route into a treacherous one. As they rounded a bend Ken felt the car tilt towards the river a hundred feet below. In the split second that Ken had for thought, those adverts for Land Rover, which show the vehicle's ability to negotiate slopes of forty five degrees, flashed through his mind. He pulled hard on the steering wheel with the improbable hope of somehow actually driving this Land Rover and his passengers safely back onto the narrow road.

Ken's effort was, unfortunately, to no avail. The soft soil just gave way and the vehicle began rolling. As they rolled down the hill Ken banged his head and was knocked unconscious. One of the passengers, Eila, also had a thought flashing through her mind. She was wondering why the trees they were hitting weren't stopping the vehicle from rolling. This was because they were banana trees which don't have a solid trunk. The tumbling Land Rover ploughed them down. They may have had a slowing effect on their descent and prevented the vehicle's downward progress from reaching what could easily have become a fatal speed. However, it certainly didn't seem that way to anyone in the vehicle!

Another passenger, John, whose mind was also working at lightning speed, even managed to count the number of rolls the vehicle made, which was approximately five. When halfway down the hill the Land Rover hit a log, which is far more substantial than a banana tree, and the three passengers in the rear were thrown out of the back. The passengers, together with the rear door, went flying. Miraculously, the mother with a small baby on her lap was found sitting under a banana tree with the baby, unhurt, still on her lap!

The Land Rover finally came to rest on its roof in a shallow stream at the bottom of the hill. Ken regained consciousness and found himself on the passenger side, up against John who had been sitting there. Eila was sprawled across the roof, which was partly underwater, with the wheel arches above her. Ken and John managed to crawl out of the small sliding window into the mud. John pulled the window right out and then they managed to pull Eila out and had her carried up the hill by some of the local people who were gathering round. They took out all the baggage, removed the wheels and sent everything up to the road with the help of some of the onlookers. Nothing went missing; even a small calculator was safely returned to the church. Everyone had survived with only cuts and bruises. That Land Rover was one of twelve that Ken shipped from England to Mombasa and driven through to Rwanda. It was a sorry sight upside down in the stream with its wheels missing and no glass left in the windows.

Rwanda is such a densely populated small country, that there were a lot of local people who heard the drumming sound of the Land Rover tumbling down the hillside. A crowd soon gathered from the surrounding community. On seeing everyone alive, someone remarked, 'The Lord has certainly preserved you.'

Everyone was helped to clamber back up the hill to the road. John and Eila returned to the church. Ken went with Pastor Venuste to the small local market to try to find help.

Providentially, there was a man visiting with a small motorbike. He agreed to take Ken to the Forestry Centre of Rangiro, which was run by a Swiss organisation, to look for a vehicle. Ken then travelled on the back of this motorbike for thirteen kilometres on the muddy track, with one foot on the only footrest and the other held out awkwardly away from the wheel. He had rescued his cameras and had one on each shoulder. The driver was wearing a large Stetson hat and Ken had to keep his head away from it. It was a very uncomfortable journey!

They finally arrived at the forestry centre and found a small Suzuki pick-up which the manager agreed to send back to the church for John, Eila and all the gear. The driver reached the place where the road had given way and saw the Land Rover upside down in the stream below. He called for people with their implements (African hoes), and with their help cut further into the hillside to widen the road.

The Pastor, (who later became the Bishop of Butare), decided that he and the two passengers would stay at the church and sent Ken, John and Eila on with the camp beds, sleeping bags etc. They were taken to a hospital at Kibogora which was run by the American 'Free Methodist' Mission, where they were patched up. The next day Ken borrowed a car and drove with John to the missionary conference centre, called Kumbya, on Lake Kivu. Eila was kept in the hospital for two days to allow her to recover for a little longer.

The reason the Pastor and his Catechist had been in the car was that they were planning to baptise John to signify his fresh start. Now Ken did it by himself. They put on their swimming trunks and waded into Lake Kivu and John was baptised by full immersion. John had never been baptised as a baby. It was a momentous experience for both of them.

John announced that the dark sins of his past life now lay at the bottom of Lake Kivu. They both felt they had escaped death by God's grace and the Lord had work for them to do. So they both dedicated their lives afresh to His service.

When Ken finally arrived home to his parish of Penhurst, the churchwarden, Paul Broomhall, who himself was from a missionary family, told Ken that when he heard the report of the accident he had said, 'We can't let the work stop because of the accident, we must buy another vehicle.' In no time at all, he had put together enough funds for him to present Ken with a similar blue Land Rover.

Ken shipped the replacement out with tools and a spare new battery for his next visit, and having negotiated the customs at Mombasa and the borders of Kenya/Uganda, then Uganda/Rwanda, drove it through the Nyungwe Forest to Banda. He took with him an engineer, Patrick Foss-Smith, from the organisation 'Christian Engineers in Development' (see www.ced.org.uk). Patrick inspected the sorry sight of Ken's damaged Land Rover with no glass and the bodywork bent and leaning to one side, which was by then, back at the village. Before they had left the village, six months previously, Ken had sent a note to the local Chief to tell him what had happened.

Taking the initiative, the Chief had sent a large group of his men to the stricken Land Rover. The wheels were retrieved from the village and replaced on the vehicle before it was turned the right way up. The men carried the Land Rover (which weighed close to two tons) along the river bed and up to the church. It sat there for six months and nothing was touched. Patrick the engineer, started work on the crumpled heap. He took the engine oil out of the cylinders, cleaned anything that needed cleaning in the engine and attached the new battery using 'bulldog clips'. Within a few hours, to the amazement of Patrick's enraptured audience of local villagers, the engine spluttered and started. He then drove it round the compound with a great crowd of excited children following.

The Landrover recovered from the valley

They strapped up the body with ropes and drove very carefully in convoy up through the forest to Butare where Ken was based. There was no hope for the rear of the Land Rover bodywork. However, Ken had the top half of the vehicle's body removed, converting it into a useful pick-up. He left it for Pastor Venuste to use, who eventually ruined the engine by failing to replenish the engine oil or topping up the water in the radiator – a very African story!

The main road was by then, almost completed by Chinese workers. Teams of workers from China lived for some months in temporary cabins to supervise the building and tarmacing of the road which went from Butare to Cyangugu. This was part of a programme of major roads across the country connecting border posts of Uganda in the north, Burundi in the south, Zaire in the south-west and Tanzania to the east, and to Kigali, the capital of Rwanda, where all the government ministries were based.

African adventures such as this one, involved pain, discomfort and stress. However, they were also a powerful reminder to Ken of God's sovereign care and guidance in times of danger and uncertainty. God was certainly with him in the good times, and in the difficult ones too.

*   *   *

Ken was never one to take himself too seriously and the members of his congregation often saw his lighter side and good sense of humour. In one service in Ashburnham in 1984, he arrived back from one of his African trips on the day before his birthday, which was on the Sunday. Jill had been visiting in the parish and had told some of the villagers that if they wanted to give the vicar a welcome back then they should come to church on his birthday.

Ken put on his clerical robes as usual and walked into the chancel. To his surprise, the organist started up with 'Happy Birthday to you...etc'. Ken was a bit taken aback; this was just not normal for an Anglican service. He looked at the congregation and saw that it was a full church with many parishioners who weren't often there. The special invitations from Jill had brought in the additional people. With an appreciative smile on his face, Ken announced the first hymn and began singing it with his usual great gusto as the adrenaline pumped. Suddenly, his front tooth fell out! It was an old rugby break which had been crowned. Ken crumpled with laughter and tried to hide behind his hymn book. At the end of the hymn Ken had to own up to what had just happened. There was laughter and a wonderful spirit in the service as the congregation enjoyed his misfortune. Jill had had a large birthday cake made and everyone had a piece as they went out from a very warm service. It was a service that was destined to live in the memory of the congregation for Ken's juggling with his tooth rather than anything he might have preached afterwards!

CHAPTER TWELVE

Consecration

In 1992 Ken was making one of his regular visits to clergy in Rwanda. He went to the rural parish of Nyarusange, which was the only church in the diocese to have a brick built house for the pastor. It had been built by Ken's builder some years before it became part of Cyangugu Diocese. Bishop Daniel Nduhura, newly appointed as Bishop of Cyangugu, had taken up residence in the pastor's house. He told Ken that there was no way he could develop a diocese with only three mud built rural churches and nothing whatsoever in the town. He couldn't drive and his driver had left him. He had no staff, as the man he brought with him as Diocesan Secretary had also left, and he had no money and no salary. How could he possibly develop a new diocese in the most remote part of the country? He asked Ken if he would come and join him as Assistant Bishop, hoping that this would generate some practical help and income from abroad.

The first step would be to consult the Rwanda House of Bishops. They were unsure if it was possible for Ken to be an Assistant Bishop in Rwanda and a parish vicar in England at the same time. They wanted to know what the Church of England would think and asked Ken to enquire from Chichester Diocese and the Archbishop of Canterbury Dr George Carey, for whom they had great respect. Ken was back in England at this time and went to see Archbishop Carey, who was quite happy with the proposed arrangement and provided Ken with a letter confirming this. The Bishop of Chichester and the Area Bishop of Lewes also agreed and wrote approvingly, seeing it as a way of helping the Church in Rwanda to cope with a problem.

So on 7th June 1993 Ken flew out to Rwanda and handed the three letters to the Archbishop of Rwanda. The Bishops then agreed with Bishop Daniel's request. Ken was to continue his work in the parishes of Ashburnham and Penhurst and go to Rwanda for a month twice a year to help Bishop Daniel to develop the diocese. In the Anglican Communion rules, once he was Consecrated as a Bishop in Rwanda, he would be in that order within the whole worldwide Anglican Communion, for life. It was a major development in his ministry and would prove to be very useful later.

Cyangugu is in the remote southwest area of Rwanda and had been cut off by the large area of natural Forest of Nyungwe, through which there was no proper road. The area had been left behind during the development of the country in the 1960s. When the CMS missionaries finally had permission to set up church centres (called mission stations at that time) in Ruanda-Urundi in the 1920's they didn't reach Cyangugu at all. So there had never been any Anglican church in the area until 1977 when it became part of the Diocese of Butare in the south. Now the Bishops had approved the appointment and set a date, it was left to Ken to make the arrangements for his consecration service.

It is hard to envisage a diocesan centre without a single building. No church, house, congregation or pastor! The Presbyterian Church, which had been established many years before, agreed that their choir would form a committee to prepare for the consecration service. The only place in Cyangugu which would hold a crowd was the football stadium. Ken was granted a three month sabbatical by his Chichester Diocese and this allowed time for the preparations.

Africans love a ceremony and the bigger the better. With the venue settled, arrangements had to be made to bring poles and boards for the Presbyterian choir to build a podium in the middle of the stadium. Ken purchased some bulls to be slaughtered and cooked as part of the feeding of a thousand guests. Special seating had to be provided for VIPs and invitations were printed and distributed. The choir did all this in June and July and everything was ready for the special and sacred service on August 22nd 1993.

On 7th June 1993 Ken flew to Kigali for his three month stay. Important events were planned for this trip. Immediately after his consecration ceremony, Ken was to be the keynote speaker at a large convention in Kisoro, which was across the border in Uganda. Delegates would attend from many places including the United States.

On arrival in Kigali, Ken picked up his Land Rover which had been looked after by the American Ambassador at his residence. He drove to his house in Butare. He had planned to send Bishop Daniel to a language school in Hove in the UK, to improve his knowledge of English. While Daniel was away, Ken was intending to start the planned building programme in the diocese of Cyangugu. Ken's brother Peter sent his son Douglas to help with the development work.

On 14th June 1993 Ken set out to drive Bishop Daniel from Cyangugu to Kigali, a six hour journey in his Series 3 Land Rover, to obtain a passport for Daniel's visit to England. Half way to Kigali they called in at Shyogwe, one of the diocesan centres to see the Bishop, Samuel Musabyimana. It would be a detour not far off their route, so it was a good opportunity to see him. They left Cyangugu in good time to complete the drive to Kigali before dark. Driving in the dark could be difficult and dangerous, so it was avoided if at all possible. As they reached the local market just outside the town they came to a halt; a tree lay right across the road. Suspecting that it had been put there deliberately to block the way, Ken tried to reverse out of the situation, only to find that another tree had been pushed behind them. It was a trap.

A very nasty scene ensued as a large, noisy crowd quickly surrounded them and began beating on the vehicle. To make matters worse, many of them appeared to be drunk and were dancing and waving their Primus beer bottles around. It was a very frightening situation. They were also trying to damage the vehicle by pulling bits off it. Some of the crowd were trying to open the door where Bishop Daniel sat in stunned silence in the front passenger seat and possibly wondering if this was the time that he would be meeting his Maker. It was Bishop Daniel who was the centre of their anger; he owed money to a lot of local people.

The instigator of this action was Bishop Daniel's former driver François. He lived in the area of Shyogwe and had driven the Bishop down to Cyangugu about a month earlier. Daniel had never himself learned to drive. Daniel had not paid him and after some days he had given up and left Cyangugu to return to his home in Shyogwe feeling angry and cheated. Then he heard that Bishop Daniel was coming to Shyogwe to visit Bishop Musabyimana who also lived there. He gathered a crowd and waited for Bishop Daniel's arrival to spring the trap and exact his revenge on the Bishop by giving him a good beating.

Ken opened his window and began asking some of the crowd what the problem was, in an attempt to negotiate their way out of this dangerous situation. He wasn't getting much sense from any of them other than 'He owes us money!' Someone from the local congregation must have run the short distance back to the village to alert Bishop Musabyimana about the situation and to telephone the local gendarmerie, who appeared on the scene very quickly. They came with guns at the ready and prepared to use them to rescue Ken and Bishop Daniel. Soon Bishop Musabyimana arrived by car and bravely pushed his way through the crowd where he was roughed up by some of the thugs for his trouble.

The Bishop's immediate task was to restrain the gendarmes from shooting anyone and calm everyone down. He arrived at the car window looking dishevelled after making his way through the hostile crowd. Once a relative calm had been established, it was then time to begin the negotiations that hopefully would bring the whole episode to a conclusion without anyone getting hurt.

The police officer in charge, Bishop Musabyimana, (standing by Ken's window), and Ken, still sitting in the driver's seat, negotiated with members of the crowd over the next four hours. There was a line of people who had worked for Bishop Daniel complaining he had not paid them. The process became like a mini court of enquiry. Ken, Bishop Musabyimana and the senior officer together, had to determine who had genuine claims from those making false ones and listing them all. Only then was the crowd willing to disperse, on the understanding that they would all be paid in the morning. Ken's promise was the important factor in all this. The villagers had confidence that the 'muzungu' would have access to the money to settle the debts, and moreover he was unlikely to break his promise. The next day Ken paid all the claimants that were considered genuine and the total cost to him was £1,250. Sadly, this came out of the money he had taken for building work.

Ken and Daniel eventually travelled to Kigali on 22 June for Daniel to catch his flight to England. Meanwhile, on the same day, the Rwanda House of Bishops met to decide that the date of Ken's consecration would be 22nd August – not realising the problem this date would give Ken.

Back in Cyangugu Ken took possession of a house in Cyangugu for Bishop Daniel to live in after his return from England. Ken rented it from an Omani Arab, and paid two years rent in advance. At that stage Ken had no building of any sort in the town of Cyangugu in which to hold services. As a temporary measure he rented a chapel from the Roman Catholic parish and arranged a conference for the only three pastors in the diocese and the church catechists, in Cyangugu, from 28th to 30th June. Instructors for the conference included Silas Sebera from the Christian Rural Service and Archdeacon Festo Gakware from Butare. (Both were tragically killed in the genocide the following year).

On 10th August, some friends and family of Ken's were able to join him in Rwanda to share the occasion of Ken's consecration. Jill arrived in Kigali on Ethiopian Airways from London with their daughter Sue and her husband Ken, together with the Revd Garry Guinness and his wife Jeannette and Bishop Daniel, back from his English study in Hove. On 15th August their daughter Jane arrived from Somalia, where she was working with the International Rescue Committee.

It is in the nature of Africans, that when your leader is honoured, everyone feels honoured. The celebration is for everyone and usually a grand time is had by all. All eight members of the Rwanda House of Bishops and the four from Uganda, Burundi and Zaire arrived in Cyangugu and Ken was responsible for accommodating and feeding them all. Ken, recognising that this call had actually come from God, was happy to take on the task. Thus it was, in a celebratory atmosphere the solemn part of the proceedings came when all the Bishops laid their hands on Ken, and he was consecrated as a Bishop of the Anglican Church with the specific role of assisting Bishop Daniel to develop the diocese of Cyangugu.

*   *   *

The longest day

Ken faced two main obstacles: firstly, the time gap between the two events was short. Secondly, to reach Kisoro in time for the convention where he was the speaker, he needed to transit the north eastern area of Rwanda, which, after two and a half years of fighting, was under the control of the Rwanda Patriotic Front (RPF) who had invaded from Uganda. The alternative route at this time was to go through Kigali and take the road up to Kampala and then back down to the south west of Uganda to Kisoro, thus avoiding the RPF held area of Rwanda. That area was tense at best and very dangerous at worst. This safer but longer route would take several days. The border with Uganda was closed and peace talks were in process at Arusha in Tanzania. The only way Ken could get to Kisoro in time for the convention was to go through RPF held territory to the border crossing at Cyanika. From this crossing it was a short journey to Kisoro.

Ken had not had any control of the timing of either event. To attempt to participate in both these events was going to be very difficult to manage. However, he was never the one to duck a challenge and he really felt that if the Lord wanted Jill and himself to be at both, it could be managed. First he consulted an officer of the RPF, Commander Birasa, who was staying at the Meridian Hotel in Kigali as part of the peace negotiations. He agreed that Ken and Jill could go through that area if they were escorted by a detachment from the UN peace keeping force. He told Ken where he could find the UN base for that area, and advised he should write to the Minister of the Interior for permission to have a UN escort.

Back at Cyangugu he began the process by faxing a letter to the Minister, and then continued with the preparations for the consecration ceremony in the football stadium hoping that the letter would pave the way for the trip to Kisoro. On 25th August, the day before the convention, Ken and Jill set out early on the drive north. They found the place where the UN were stationed and contacted the Senegalese officer in charge. The officer stated he couldn't give them an escort without a letter from the Minister. Disappointed but determined, Ken drove back through all the government roadblocks to Kigali.

In an effort to look as official and impressive as possible, Ken had his 'Episcopal flag' flying on the old Land Rover. It would have looked more at home fluttering from the bonnet of a Mercedes limousine, but the Land Rover would have to do. This flag was white with a Christian cross in red and had the letters EER in one quarter. It had been made by their daughter Sue before the trip. They hoped that this plus Ken's diplomatic passport would be intimidating enough for any official to let them pass with a salute and a cheery smile. However, as so often happens in Africa, caution and bureaucracy won the day.

They reached the appropriate Ministry by 11.55am, conscious that Rwandan officialdom had inherited the disastrous Gallic system of a two hour lunchtime which began at midday. Using his brand new purple Bishop's shirt and clerical collar as a display of authority, Ken managed to gatecrash the normal obstacle course of bureaucratic protocol and marched into the Minister's office just before 12.00, leaving a string of slightly confused minor functionaries in his wake. Ken told his story to the Minister who asked him if he had written asking for permission to have an escort. Ken explained that he had indeed sent a fax. The Minister searched for the fax among the various piles of papers that can be seen on the desk of all government officials just about anywhere in Africa; but he failed to find any record of it.

Ken told him that he had given a copy to the Prefect (Governor) of Cyangugu. Wanting to be as helpful as possible, the Minister phoned the Prefect and asked if this was true. The Prefect confirmed that he had the letter on his desk and would fax it to the Ministry immediately. The fax came through, the Minister gave written and signed permission and by 1.00pm, with thanks, smiles and handshakes all round Ken and Jill were on their way once again back up north.

With the aid of the Episcopal flag, clerical dress and Ken's knowledge of the local languages, they were able to breeze through the government roadblocks again and arrived back at the UN by 3.00pm expecting that now they would be able to continue. However, the Senegalese officer informed them that the vehicles which would have formed their escort had gone and they would have to come back the next day.

Ken explained to him that this was not possible because the Convention was due to be opened by His Excellency Yoweri Museveni the President of Uganda and that Ken was the keynote speaker. The officer might – with some hesitation – have been prepared to block the progress of God's representative, but the prospect of disappointing the renowned President Yoweri Museveni of neighbouring Uganda, brought authority to bear on the situation that was much too close to home for comfort and he said that they could pass, but it would be without an escort.

It had been a close call, but armed with the ministerial letter, they were now on their way. As they drove they became very aware that they were now travelling through what was then rebel held territory. They travelled mile after mile through the bush without seeing a soul. It was eerie, a little unnerving, and in one of the most densely populated countries on Earth, unique in Ken's experience. Ken and Jill couldn't help wondering if they were being watched by rebel soldiers in the bush, but they pressed on northwards towards the border.

Suddenly, across this good tarmac road was a massive mound of earth. It was twenty five feet high and had obviously been there a long time because it had sprouted grass, bushes and small trees. Ken got out of the Land Rover and called out to see if anyone was around. There was no response. This was obviously a tactical roadblock that had been bulldozed into place by the Rwanda government more than two years previously to prevent the RPF forces or anyone else from Uganda advancing south. Again, Ken wondered if they were being watched from the bushes.

The roadblock was large, but as Ken looked at it, he wondered if the famous climbing ability of the Land Rover could actually drive over it. There was only one way to find out! Jill got out of the vehicle and Ken engaged low ratio four-wheel drive and went for a gap in the trees. The loose rocks started slipping and the Land Rover was heading for a tree. Ken had to reverse back down. Just then a woman appeared. She was friendly and seeing the situation, wanted to help. The three of them moved rocks into place to make a way up the hill that might give the vehicle enough grip. This time the Land Rover's famous low ratio and Ken's bush driving experience triumphed and he crested the artificial hill and drove gingerly down the other side. Jill clambered over on foot and climbed back into the passenger seat. The woman just disappeared as suddenly as she had arrived and they set off again towards the border.

Hardly daring to believe that anything in this part of the country was still the same, they arrived at the border crossing which was where it had always been. The one big difference was that there was no one around. It looked deserted. The customs house was empty and the large white barrier was down and appeared to be locked with a large padlock, and there was no way round it. Just then, two men appeared. They said that Ken and Jill's coming had given them courage. This may seem an odd thing to say, but the few local people remaining in that area must have felt isolated and deserted; a very strange experience for anyone in this normally crowded area. To see an English clergyman and his wife arriving at the border post just like it used to be before the fighting began must have been encouraging for them.

The men pointed out that the padlock was not through its staple. It only appeared to be locked from a distance. Ken simply lifted the barrier and they were able to pass through and replace the barrier. As in almost all inland border crossings, there was a stretch of 'no man's land'; in this case about fifty yards, to the Uganda customs post. The two men tried to follow the vehicle, but were shouted at by a border guard and sent back.

The Ugandan soldier in charge was drunk and determined not to be helpful. The combination of a soldier in authority, holding a gun and being drunk also, is a frightening prospect. Jill sat in the vehicle observing the situation and felt fearful. In fact the whole day had been a mixture of stress, frustration and fear. The soldier informed them that his commanding officer had given orders that no one was allowed into Uganda from Rwanda. The border had been shut for two and a half years and no one had crossed at all during this time. He also revealed that Bishop Ernest Shalita from Kisoro had been waiting for them for some hours on the other side but had given up and returned to Kisoro.

He kept Ken and Jill there for three hours and it was dark before he finally agreed to Ken's request that he go with them in the vehicle to find his commander. They drove to a nearby military camp where the soldier left them sitting in the vehicle while he went off to find his commander. Ken and Jill sat there in the dark, wondering what would happen next. They were in a vulnerable situation and Jill testified later that she felt terrified.

Half an hour later he came with another soldier and both of them crammed into the front seats with their AK47 rifles held at their sides and pressing into Jill's side, further reducing the available space. They were drunk and Jill desperately hoped their safety catches were on preventing the guns from accidentally firing on the bumpy road. They drove on to the town and found the commander in the video café. He came out and just said, 'No problem, you can go.' With enormous relief they became the first travellers to cross that border in two and a half years. They continued to their destination, found the church and knocked on the door. As they walked in, the organising team were actually praying, 'that Bishop Ken would get here somehow.' They looked up to see the answer to their prayers! There was great rejoicing all round and thanks to God. The tension of this exceptionally stressful day was lifted. It is hard to imagine anyone else even trying to do what Ken and Jill had succeeded in doing that day. God had honoured their faith and determination – it had been a very long day! Many other wives would have demanded that they turn round and abandon the trip because it was just too difficult and dangerous. The Convention went ahead the next day as planned and Ken completed his talks on the Prophet Hosea.

At the end of the Convention they were escorted to the border by Bishop Shalita and the police. This time they passed straight through the Ugandan border post. They knew what to expect on the Rwanda side and lifted the barrier easily then passed the customs house without seeing a soul. Once again they negotiated the large mound in the vehicle's four wheel drive low ratio gear, then the government road blocks, before continuing on the mountain road from the northern town of Ruhengeri towards Kigali. They stopped for a moment of prayer and a banana, giving thanks for an easy return journey.

Further down the road they were halted behind a line of stationary cars and they could see that at the head of the line there was a tree across the road. This is not unusual because trees were often blown down in storms. To cope with this problem, African truck drivers usually carry an axe and accept chopping up and removing fallen trees as part of the job and usually become very skilled in this task. Ken and Jill just waited for the men to come with their axes to remove it from the road. Instead, a very angry young man came up to their vehicle. Ken asked him what the problem was and he said, 'We are hungry. The food from the trucks has been taken by "the big people" and we are hungry.'

Ken asked how he could help, and he replied 'A thousand francs.'

Ken realised that these men had set up their own unofficial road tax points to solve the problem of having their food allocation stolen by corrupt officials. He handed the man the money and he shouted down the line, 'Let this one through.' However, it was not down the tarmac road that they were let through to, but down a small bush track into a valley. The Land Rover coped with the road easily enough, but lower down the valley they came to a small bridge with another group of angry young men. This time, one hundred Rwanda francs were enough for the men to replace the poles back on the bridge and let them through.

Further along the road there was another bridge and a crowd of young men. This time Ken simply handed out a hundred francs, but they shouted at him, 'Five hundred francs!' As they drove on in the direction of Kigali they passed by a large camp for internally displaced people (IDPs). They concluded that this was where these young men had come from and from where the food had been stolen by 'big people'. In Kigali they reported the incident to a gendarme, who showed no interest at all.

The final convention meeting was on Sunday 29th. Sue flew back home that day from Kigali, Jill flew back on 4th September and Ken returned on 21st September to carry on his parish work in the UK.

It had been a memorable trip to say the least. On his first Sunday back in the church at Ashburnham, Ken was given a loud cheer as he walked out of the vestry in his new Episcopal robes. It was a wonderful occasion.

It is one of God's ironies that Ken, who as a young man, didn't want to be a clergyman, and wanted to live in Africa, not England, was now an Anglican Bishop in both places! Ken thought that everything was now set for him to launch into a new phase of his ministry. With God's help he would create a new diocese in this remote part of Rwanda that would proclaim in word and deed the love of God and the gospel of Christ. Not many people were ready for what happened next. Ken's vision would remain, and indeed the need for it become the more urgent, when on April 6th 1994 all hell broke loose in his beloved Rwanda. The world called it *'Genocide.'*

CHAPTER THIRTEEN

I *Must* Return

During April 1994, Ken's immediate reaction to the unfolding Genocide in Rwanda was an overwhelming urgency to get back as soon as he could, whatever the dangers. He had very little idea of what had happened in Cyangugu. He quickly put together a trip with two companions, Tony Isaac and Graham Turnbull. For a long time Tony had had an interest in Rwanda. His father was one of Ken's trustees and his grandfather had worked with Ken's father in the Ruanda Mission. Graham was a practicing lawyer in the north of England and had become interested in Rwanda through the publicity put out by Ken as part of his work with the Rwanda Mission. He too had been glued to the news reports from Rwanda and wanted to try to do something to help in any way that he could. He rang Ken one day and asked about the possibility of going to Rwanda. Graham had also taken the time to do a TEFL course (teaching English as a Foreign Language), always a very useful skill to have for anyone interested in serving overseas.

Being a lawyer, he was interested in the legal aspects of the Genocide as well as a humanitarian crisis. He offered to go and teach English while he was there. Having reviewed their travel options they decided it was far easier and safer if they could cross the border from the Democratic Republic of Congo (DCR), entering from the south near Cyangugu. It was a big decision to go at this time. No one knew how long the killing would continue. There were still six weeks to go before the Rwandan Patriotic Front forces, under the command of Paul Kagame entered Kigali and began to restore law and order on July 4th. Ken purchased a Land Rover in Heathfield, East Sussex and shipped it to Mombasa, the main port in Kenya. Allowing time for the vehicle to arrive in Mombasa by sea, a month later they flew to Kenya and cleared their vehicle through the port.

Ken needed some God-given courage to make this trip. Not many people wanted to go to Rwanda at this time. Jill also needed God's courage to be the one staying at home praying, and not knowing what was going on. She had become accustomed to his many trips to Rwanda and while he was away she often spent the time raising funds in whatever way she could.

"Please read me a story, Granny"

She occupied her time – and importantly on this occasion – her mind, organising sponsorship events, visiting other clergy they knew and, with a smile on her face, she put the case for supporting the work. This trip however, was different – very different. Ken was heading into a war zone. The television reports had given them some idea of what was happening and it was very unpleasant indeed. Before departure they made sure of prayer support from all the churches in their Deanery. Jill was convinced that Ken was doing what God had called him to do and this gave her confidence that God would look after him. She had also been with Ken on some of his trips so Africa was not the dark, mysterious and forbidding place it may have been to someone who had never been there. Even so, it was not easy for her to drive Ken to Heathrow airport and wave him off into the final weeks of the Genocide.

They drove through Kenya, staying one night with Ken's cousin Philip Leakey in Nairobi. Their journey continued northwest to the border crossing into Uganda. Once in Uganda they headed southeast, skirting the northern shore of Lake Victoria to Entebbe. Here they left the Land Rover safely with a friend, George Lutaya-Kamya. He had ten children, and Ken baptised the tenth child in their own language of Luganda. They had booked a charter flight with The Missionary Aviation Fellowship (MAF) to fly to Bukavu, in Zaire on June 23rd 1994. They now assumed that they would be within easy reach of Cyangugu once they landed. They were naturally apprehensive about the situation that they might find in Cyangugu, but their long journey was nearly over. They were actually in the air when the MAF pilot informed them that the control tower in Bukavu had refused them permission to land. They later discovered the reason – the French had arrived!

Their MAF pilot had to immediately re-route to the MAF base at Nyankunde, further north on the eastern side of Zaire. They had to land at Bunia first for the formalities of clearing immigration and customs, before the short hop to the Nyankunde base where MAF had six planes. Sadly, in 2002 this base was destroyed as the Congo descended into the lawless and chaotic condition of what is sometimes called a 'failed state'. This sad title describes a country where the rule of the government does not extend throughout its land. There is no law and order, the army and the police are utterly corrupt. There are no schools, no tax or customs duty collected and the road system falls apart through lack of maintenance and heavy rains. The population live in fear of violence, rape, robbery, beatings, torture and death.

There they met a group of Rwandans who had been flown out in a military helicopter, organized by the Anglican Bishop of Shyogwe, Samuel Musabyimana. He was close to some members of the government and was able to hire one of the government's helicopters. Samuel's is a very sad story. He went from Zaire to Kenya with his doctor wife and two children and settled in Nairobi. While there, both children became ill and died. The Bishop was later arrested in South Africa where he was allegedly selling false passports to guilty Rwandans who wanted a new identity or to escape. He was indicted by the International Genocide Tribunal at Arusha in Tanzania where he later died before his trial.

The stories that Ken was picking up along the way, confirmed his worst fears. The news reports he had watched so avidly were not exaggerating the situation at all. In fact, when the multitude of stories came to light in the months and years ahead, and investigated by the Genocide Tribunal, they proved that what had happened in Rwanda was worse that anyone could have imagined.

The French were arriving by air with fighter and transport planes and troops that day; 23rd June 1994, for their 'Operation Turquoise'. They had sent their French Foreign Legion – renowned throughout their long history for their toughness and discipline. Their *'Cordon sanitaire'* prevented anyone coming in or out of the southern area without their permission. However, Rwanda and the rest of the world were soon to discover that the elite force of the French Foreign Legion were not all their reputation would have everyone believe them to be.

Tony, Graham and Ken were flown back to Entebbe in Uganda where they picked up the Land Rover and drove to Kisoro on the Ugandan side of the border with Rwanda in a second attempt to gain access. This route was also blocked; this time by the UN who were using helicopters to patrol the border, and they were forbidden to cross. They were close enough to listen to the 'hate radio' telling the people to 'deal with the cockroaches otherwise they would suffer.' The broadcasters were still pretending that they were in Kigali and everything was normal. Graham stayed on at Kisoro and taught English for six months. Ken left the Land Rover for Graham to use. Ken and Tony returned to England. On 4th July after the RPF had taken Kigali, Graham courageously headed there himself. The first real solid news of the situation came to Ken from Graham, by phone.

Sadly, in February 1997 Graham Turnbull gave his life for the cause he was so committed to. He had continued his interest in Rwanda and was working as a monitor for the United Nations Human Rights Commission in Kigali. He was asked to go to Cyangugu as part of his work. While travelling through the dense forest in south western Rwanda, the team was attacked and all but one killed by bandits left over from the Genocide. Graham was only thirty seven years old. The British Law Society now holds an annual essay competition for law students in his memory.

*   *   *

Returning to Cyangugu

Ken had been wondering how he could return to Cyangugu, when God, who can solve any problem, stepped in with an amazing provision. Ken's daughter Jane, aged twenty seven at that time, was working for the International Rescue Committee (IRC). She had been with them in Somalia until the American troops were pulled out from there in March 1994.

The Clinton administration had concluded that their mission in Somalia was virtually impossible and he decided to cut their losses and withdraw. A major contributing factor to his decision was the poorly planned American action in Mogadishu on 3rd November 1993 in which eighteen Americans were killed and seventy three wounded. There were hundreds of Somali casualties. The action became widely publicised through the Ridley Scott film 'Black Hawk Down', which American soldiers involved have confirmed was an accurate depiction of the events.

The United Nations pulled all their personnel out, including their IRC partners. When Ken heard that Jane would be re-deployed to Cyangugu with the IRC in September 1994, he asked if he could hitch a ride with them and they agreed. There were no commercial flights immediately after the genocide, so this was God's way of getting Ken not only back into Rwanda, but right to the very place he needed to go.

Naturally he was anxious to see what had been happening in Cyangugu. Were his friends safe? What had happened to Bishop Daniel? Had the horrors that had descended on the rest of Rwanda, also taken their toll in his beloved Cyangugu? The small IRC chartered aircraft had taken them from Wilson Airport in Nairobi to Kigali, where they unloaded supplies for the local IRC team straight into their car on the tarmac. In those early post-genocide days of recovery, there were no normal customs at the airport. It was controlled by RPF soldiers and officials. The IRC was widely recognised as a group who were there to help the recovery.

They then flew on to the airstrip at Cyangugu itself. It was a light aircraft with only a few seats and Ken was crammed in with water bottles and other supplies – he was part of the cargo! Ken's heart began to beat a little faster as the small plane came into land at Cyangugu's airstrip. An IRC vehicle came and met them as they landed. After unloading everything they were taken to the IRC base which was a rented house; one of the few still intact enough to be lived in.

For the next month, Ken lived in a tent pitched behind the house, which, to his delight, was the one he had rented in 1993 for the family at the time of his consecration. The IRC fed him and generally treated him as one of the team. They were, after all, there for the same purpose of bringing this traumatised town back to life.

Ken was then able to go with Jane in the IRC vehicle to cross into Congo and retrieve his Land Rover from Bukavu where it had been taken by Bishop Daniel. Ken drove the vehicle back across the Congo/Rwanda border, which was understandably very tense at that time. Masses of Hutu refugees and their leaders were fleeing from the retribution they mistakenly believed was coming. They were encouraged in this fear by their leaders, many of whom were among the guiltiest perpetrators of the genocide. Those who instigated and led the Interahamwe were in no mood to accept defeat gracefully!

The RPF forces were in control of Kigali and much of the rest of the country, but in the south they had to halt their progress in the face of the French Foreign Legion's 'Cordon Sanitaire'. They didn't want to pick a fight with the French, who, apart from the diplomatic implications, massively out-gunned them. By the time Ken returned to Rwanda, the

French had handed over control of the area to the United Nations, who belatedly had decided to try to do something useful. Shortly after crossing the border, Ken ran out of fuel; but at least he and his invaluable Land Rover were back safely in Rwanda.

One single shocking statistic powerfully sums up what Ken discovered on his return. In the area of Cyangugu alone, approximately one hundred thousand Tutsis had been killed, some while the French stood by refusing to intervene. They could have prevented most of the killing, but they didn't. The Interahamwe had the double security of knowing that the RPF could not reach them and that the French Foreign Legion was obviously going to permit them to continue the Genocide. They also knew that Kigali was a long way away and they were close to the sanctuary of the Congo border.

Ken immediately saw that almost every house in the town had been looted. Not just the items inside the houses, but all had lost their roof, doors and window frames. The buildings that normally made up a small African town had been reduced to empty shells. This rendering of anything remotely useful, was taken out by fleeing Hutu refugee and raiding parties which crossed from the UNHCR camps in Congo and returned there, crossing the bridge to Bukavu with their loot carried on their heads. This comprehensive looting took place under the indifferent gaze of the French soldiers. The French Foreign Legion was then replaced by an Ethiopian contingent of the United Nations.

Ken's own house which he used when visiting and a three-classroom school that he had built were in a similar condition. The school had also served as a small church building. When Ken had crossed over to Zaire with Jane to retrieve his vehicle, there were doors, windows and roofing sheets for sale all along the road. A refugee from Ken's own congregation reported that she had seen Ken's cupboard and blankets for sale at the roadside. Anyone in Cyangugu at this time could see ghastly reminders of what had happened there. Scores of dead bodies, many horribly mutilated and rotting were still scattered over the hillside at the back of the IRC house. However, anyone who knows him, will not be surprised that the sadness of seeing all this devastation, was soon replaced by his determination to do his best, with God's help, to put things right.

Bukavu was now bulging with Rwandan refugees and stacked with goods looted from Cyangugu. The refugee camps, all along the western and northern shores of Lake Kivu were largely controlled by the leaders of the genocidal killers, until October 1996 when the forces seeking to oust President Sese Seko Mobutu swept north destroying the camps and sending the refugees either west into the forest or north towards Goma and Kisangani. This area of Western Congo has remained a nightmarish mixture of local wars, humanitarian disasters and roaming gangs who survive by attacking and robbing the villages of the forest. Rape is endemic and no one is safe. A whole generation of young men now know no other way of life but robbing, raping and killing. Instead of raising families, crops and animals in their traditional villages and culture, they are literally raising hell. They are manipulated by various warlords, foreign business interest and ambitious politicians trying to loot Congo's natural resources of gems and minerals that should make the Congo a relatively wealthy country.

Africa is no stranger to wars and insurgencies. To help us grasp the enormity of what happened in Rwanda, we can compare it to other conflicts in that continent. Similar scenes were common in Mozambique after their civil war (1977 to 1992), but that had taken sixteen years of war with modern weapons supplied by foreign interests, to account for a million lives. In Cyangugu, there had been no war, and the devastation of the town and the appalling loss of life had all happened in a few short months. A disaster of such speed and scope, that it is probably unprecedented in modern history; and some of it happened in this particular area while a powerful and well-equipped French military force stood idly by and watched with astonishing indifference.

In this immediate aftermath of the Genocide, most of the previous inhabitants of the area had fled or been killed. For the few who had remained or returned, it must have been a relief not to be asked if they were Hutu or Tutsi. In that aspect at least, things were changing immediately for the better. Bishop Daniel had fled and this left a vacuum in spiritual leadership that the Anglican Church in Rwanda was going to need to address.

Bishop Daniel Nduhura was a Hutu, though he actually looked like a Tutsi. This almost cost Daniel and his family their lives and underlines the fact that physical appearance is not a reliable way of deciding which ethnic group a Rwandan belongs to. One of the slogans on the hate radio was 'deal with those tall people.' Height was one of the features the Belgian colonial administration considered, along with the shape of their noses and the number of cows they owned, when they introduced the identity cards which categorised the population into such groups.

During the atrocities, on one occasion Daniel and his family were travelling in a car near their village, called Gikongoro, when a gang of Hutu killers stopped them. They would have killed them, but Daniel immediately protested that they were Hutus and quickly produced his identity card which showed that this to be true. The killers were still not convinced, as false identity cards could be obtained for a bribe; they were suspicious that these may have been a forgery and they were not in the mood to give anyone the benefit of the doubt! It's likely they were eagerly eying the Bishop's daughter and anticipating what they might do to her. Fortunately, one of the killers recognised Bishop Daniel's daughter and told the others she had been in the same class as him at school and that she was indeed a Hutu, even though she looked even more like a Tutsi than her father. This intervention almost certainly saved Bishop Daniel's life and his daughter from multiple rape, brutal beating and death. No wonder Bishop Daniel fled.

In 1995, using the only builder left in the town of Cyangugu, whose name was Talasisi, Ken rebuilt his house and started building a church. It was to be the cathedral church for the brand new diocese and needed to be a little grander than the usual local church. With this in mind Ken designed it with a small tower. The rectangular nave was built first and then a semi-circular tower with a conical roof. Sadly, before the roof was finished, the builder was shot dead by a soldier friend of his with whom he was drinking. The soldier was arrested and taken to prison in Kigali. The builder's assistant finished off the roof and the cathedral was opened by the Prefect of Cyangugu and dedicated by the Bishop of Bukavu.

Cyangugu Cathedral

The cathedral has no fixed seats, but does have seven hundred polypropylene chairs shipped by container from the UK. The roof is not very high and is made of corrugated iron sheets bolted on to steel girders. During the hot, sunny days, it is like a giant oven, which is exacerbated by the heat generated by a large congregation. When it rains it is no use trying to preach, the drumming on the roof is all that can be heard. The only thing to do is to keep singing hymns until the rain stops, time not being a problem in Africa!

The looting ensured that there were no telephones anywhere in Cyangugu. All the cables and the equipment from the telephone exchange had also been taken across the bridge to Zaire. However, before Ken's next visit, his parish of Ashburnham bought him a satellite phone. Although costly to operate, it enabled Ken to keep in touch with the outside world. Unlike later satellite phones, which are smaller and hand-held, the early versions were the size of a small briefcase. To connect with the nearest geo-stationary satellite, the lid, which acted as a rectangular signal receiver, was tilted to the correct angle or completely detached and turned in the correct direction. The phone had an indicator to show the optimum position. They could be re-charged from a car battery. These early satellite phones used the International Marine Satellites (INMARSAT) network.

Ken saw many miracles of God supplying the considerable finances required for the extensive building programme. One of the most unusual examples came at a crucial stage in the construction of the guest house, when the money ran out. This project was important because a guest house would generate income to help with the rest of the development and the future running costs.

Ken returned to his house on this occasion and switched on the phone. To receive a good signal, it was necessary to position the phone in the middle of his lawn. He rang his bank manager at Barclays in Battle, in the UK, and asked for an advance of £30,000. Doing this today would be considered as a joke by any self-respecting bank manager! The manager said she would have to consult her colleague. As Ken waited, at £1 a minute, for her reply, he could see a black cloud coming across the lake from the mountains of Zaire. It was going to be a heavy storm; common at the time of year. If it reached the house before the call was complete, the phone would be soaked and the call terminated.

As Ken waited, he pressed the handset to his ear and watched anxiously as the storm clouds raced across the leaden sky towards him. Just as the first heavy spots of rain reached the garden, the bank manager came back on the line and, amazingly, said he could have the money! Ken quickly thanked her, grabbed the phone and ran for cover as the deluge soaked everything around.

It wasn't Ken's policy to borrow money, so on his return to the UK he and Jill began to pray for the money to pay off the loan quickly. Their daughter Jane came to the rescue and offered to lend them her savings, which they gladly accepted. Wonderfully, two large cheques arrived from someone whose name they had not heard before. This almost cleared the loan from the bank. They wondered who this was and how she knew about their projects in Rwanda. She was so keen to help that she took a job on the check-out tills at a Tesco supermarket and sent her pay packet every week until that project was completed. When it was finished, Ken informed her and she said 'I am so glad, my feet are killing me!'

Transferring funds from the UK was difficult because the banks, which had all been emptied by the previous regime, were not yet working under the new one. There was a lot of chaos to be sorted out; the relationships and trust with the international banking community took time to re-establish. At first Ken had to travel with his jacket pockets stuffed with bundles of $100 notes to change at the border. When Jill travelled with Ken she would sew the cash into her anorak pocket and not take it off until they arrived at their house in Cyangugu. People asked Ken why he didn't take his suit jacket off in the plane or when they arrived in the heat of Kigali. He couldn't tell them that the pockets were full of cash.

Later he found an Indian businessman in Kigali who would change an English cheque for Rwanda francs. This was a lot easier than US dollars and gave immediate access to funds. Without the banks, Ken had moved thousands of dollars on his person and millions of Rwanda francs in a biscuit tin under his Land Rover seat!

CHAPTER FOURTEEN

Ground Zero

On July 4th 1994, after a hundred days of Genocide, the Rwanda Patriotic Front had fought their way south and captured the capital Kigali and were making rapid progress in taking the rest of the country. The closer they came to the city, the less opposition there was. Once it became clear the RPF were going to take control of the country, the atmosphere changed dramatically. Government officials at all levels and the military officers panicked. Instead of taking the lives of others, suddenly it was the preservation of their own lives that became their priority. Their aim now was not only to escape retribution for their crimes, but to loot as much money and other valuables as possible then flee to the nearest international border looking for sanctuary.

Much of the mass exit was organised by the outgoing government. They sought safety for themselves among the vast numbers of their Hutu countrymen. Many of the Interahamwe and leading government militants sought – with some success – to continue to maintain their positions in the Hutu communities with whom they fled, particularly in Zaire (Zaire became the Democratic Republic of Congo in May 1997) refugee camps near the border such as those near Goma and Bukavu bordering Lake Kivu, where they set up a quasi-governmental structure under the noses of the UN administrators. The refugee leaders were frustrated, realising their Genocidal plan would have worked if the RPF had not been so quick and effective in their military advance. Some even entertained the misguided notion that they could do what Paul Kagame had done and prepare an army in exile to return one day and repeat the awful cycle of death.

Well over a million Hutu Rwandans fled southwest and crossed into Zaire – where the UNHCR set up some of the largest refugee camps the world has seen, along the shores of Lake Kivu – or retreated east into Tanzania. Most of the Interahamwe and many ordinary Hutu citizens now expected the RPF and any Tutsis left alive, to take their revenge. In fact they expected Genocide in reverse, with masses of Hutus being slaughtered. As things turned out, this didn't happen, but it is reasonable to see why they thought it would.

In the first three months after the original exodus, about 140,000 refugees had returned to Rwanda, mostly by their own choice. Once they heard that the rumours of mass revenge killings the Interahamwe had told them would surely take place, were just propaganda and not reality, most simply wanted to go home and hopefully get on with whatever their lives had once been.

The rate of exile was unprecedented in modern times. An estimated 500,000 Rwandans fled east into Tanzania by the end of May. Driven by fear of what the RPF might do as its forces swept south and east, 250,000 people crossed the bridge at Rusumo Falls into Ngara in Tanzania in 24 hours, in what the UNHCR agency called 'the largest and fastest refugee exodus in modern times'. The apparent organisation of the evacuation at Rusumo is seen as evidence that the collapsing government was behind the large refugee outflows. By May 1994, a further 200,000 people from the provinces of Butare, Kibungo, and Kigali-Rural had fled south into Burundi. By the end of August, UNHCR estimated that there were 2.1 million Rwandan refugees in neighbouring countries located in 35 camps. Other estimates are larger. Joël Boutroue, a senior UNHCR staff member in the refugee camps, wrote: *'Discussions with refugee leaders showed that exile was the continuation of war by other means.'*

The French soon ended their intervention, leading to the flight of a further 300,000 people from the 'Zone Turquoise' west towards the Zairean town of Bukavu. On 18 July 1994, RPF forces – having occupied Kigali, the capital – captured the north-western town of Gisenyi and declared a new government with Pasteur Bizimungu as president and Paul Kagame in the newly-created position of vice-president. The fall of Gisenyi caused over 800,000 Rwandans to cross into Goma, Zaire, in just four days in late July. This outflow was also highly organized, with administrative structures simply transferred across the border.

The new population around Goma included 30,000 to 40,000 soldiers of the former regular army of Rwanda. They were fully armed with an intact officer corps and a transport unit. Among these were most of the politicians. The only other camp complex to host significant numbers of leaders was the large Benaco camp in Tanzania, which held a small number of the exiled military and political leadership. The exiles chose to base themselves mainly in Zaire because of the support given by the President, Mobuto Sese Seko. The five camps around Goma, among others, eventually took on an air of permanence, eventually containing 2,323 bars, 450 restaurants, 589 shops, 62 hairdressers, 51 pharmacies, 30 tailors, 25 butchers, five ironsmiths and mechanics workshops, four photo studios, three movie theatres, two hotels and one slaughterhouse.

The UNHCR was forced to halt its efforts to repatriate refugees after both their staff and the refugees were threatened under the orders of the exiled Hutu leadership.

However, by September 1994 questionable or exaggerated rumours of violence by the RPF within Rwanda, combined with tightened control by the Hutu leadership of the camps, had drastically reduced the rate of return and eventually stopped it altogether by early 1995.

While the French soldiers were in Cyangugu, bands of refugees came back across the border and stripped anything that had not already been taken as Hutus hurriedly evacuated the area. Any remaining roofing sheets, doors and window frames were wrenched out of the brickwork. Electrical cables were stripped from the houses and the telegraph poles. Anything that could be sold or used and could be carried was taken into Zaire.

Houses and other buildings were turned into ghostly brick skeletons. Lindsey Hilsum, a journalist reporting for the UK television Channel 4, in trying to describe the scene said she saw 'the whole country being carried on people's heads across the bridge to Bukavu.' This included everything from the house Ken had rented from an Arab for Bishop Daniel, as well as the small school he had just built, and even his own house.

Such a comprehensive rendering of everything with a perceived value, happened in such a short space of time, could only be accomplished by a fleeing population of hundreds of thousands. From the time the word spread that the RPF had taken Kigali and the arrival of a UN force in the southern areas of the country was only a few weeks. As with most aspects of this tragedy, everything was beyond normal comparisons in the speed, ferocity and sheer numbers of people involved.

Having failed to complete the task of totally annihilating Rwanda's Tutsi population, this was a sort of parting shot. For most of those who were now suddenly refugees, most of the items might raise pathetically small amounts of cash. Some of the materials were not perhaps for sale, but were building materials, such as doors or roof sheets that might be useful for constructing accommodation; should it be needed.

The UN was supposed to administer the refugee camps, but their control was only nominal. UN officials made no effort to prevent the activities of the leaders of the former Rwandan regime and their Interahamwe extremists from controlling and intimidating the people. Using threats and violence, they were determined to keep what they perceived as their power-base of people. Many raiding parties of Interahamwe were organised and sent back into Rwanda, often using the dense forest as cover. The aim was to destabilise the new government and the UN were unwilling or unable to tackle the problem.

The new Rwandan Ambassador to the Netherlands, Immaculee Uwanyiligira, said 'The UN and its army of NGOs which descended on Goma in 1994, woefully failed to separate real refugees from Genocidal forces, but instead continued to feed, house and nurse their forces back to health, hence unwittingly or indeed deliberately enabling and emboldening them to continue to train in full military gear and to attack Rwanda with impunity'. The French army of Operation Turquoise, which took up position in the western region on 22nd June 1994, withdrew from Rwanda in July and were replaced by UN troops from Ghana and Ethiopia. It was several years before all the people of these camps were repatriated.

*   *   *

On their arrival in Kigali, the RPF under the command of Paul Kagame, looked around them and realised – perhaps for the first time – the monumental task of nation building that they now faced. Kagame and his officers were left with a country that had no administrators, judges, courts, civil servants or even regional 'chiefs', (an important part of the administration network in most African countries). Schools were left without many of their head teachers and other staff. Kagame's soldiers and officers suddenly had a massive vacuum to fill. Soldiers had to become policemen and administrators. It was a steep learning curve.

All the money from the banks, including the National Bank, was looted by the political/military leaders and senior civil servants and taken with them to Zaire or Tanzania. The various ministry offices were stripped bare and all the government buses and official vehicles, including military ones, were taken out of Rwanda. It was *ground zero*; Rwanda was on the verge of becoming a failed state.

Now, everyone looked on and wondered what would happen next. Those who were not guilty of any violence thought that they might be blamed anyway. The Tutsis, who were in exile or had managed to hide, hoped against hope that they might be able to live safely in their own land. The world looked on in horror as the magnitude of what had happened began to unfold. Anyone who has studied the history of ethnic and tribal conflicts in Africa would assume that the situation was now ripe for revenge and would expect mass reprisals.

This did not happen in Rwanda. A surprisingly small number of local incidents were reported, but there were no mass killings. Paul Kagame's leadership was the major factor in this. Once it was realised that the new government would not be seeking revenge and that it would in fact punish anyone who tried to perpetuate the violence, whatever their ethnicity, the whole atmosphere changed and people began to feel safer. Kagame's army was more disciplined than the history of ethnic and tribal conflicts in Africa would lead anyone to expect. His people and their families had seen enough evidence of slaughter and genuinely wanted the killing to stop, or there would be no country left to live in! They genuinely wanted to live in their own land and make a new life after many years as refugees in neighbouring countries.

Reconciliation and compromise are strong characteristics of most African cultures. For centuries, disputes in villages or arguments over land, have usually been resolved by the chief, who always came up with a compromise to settle the argument. Though one party may clearly be in the wrong, they would get something out of the settlement, even if it was small, in order to allow them to save face. Everyone was expected to abide by the compromise set out by the Chief.

This was the aim of the new administration. Their country must never again be torn by ethnic division and violence. Reconciliation, forgiveness and unity were going to be the themes of the new Rwanda that would rise from the ashes of the past. Those who wished to continue the divisions would not be tolerated, the stakes were just too high to allow the historic conflict to be perpetuated in any form by anyone either within the country or abroad. Where those who had participated in the genocide could be apprehended, they would face an international standard of justice in the courts. Justice for horrific crimes would not be sacrificed, but the communities as a whole must now learn to live together in harmony as they had once done for centuries.

One of the first acts of Paul Kagame's administration was to abolish the identity cards which had been introduced by the Belgian colonial administration. The cards clearly stated that you were Hutu, Tutsi or Twa. These cards were more than administrative; they were now a stigma on the nation. They symbolised all the hatred and division that had caused so much suffering in the nation's history. New cards were issued that stated only that the holders were Rwandan. Any discrimination on ethnic grounds would now be illegal.

A civil police force would be trained to take over from the gendarmerie, which was a military police force made up from the invading RPF. This would gradually be replaced by a civilian police force which makes no distinction between ethnic groups. The international community and its institutions looked on and breathed a collective sigh or relief. Once they realised that Paul Kagame meant what he was saying and had begun the task of implementing his ideas, the international aid began to flow. As the Bible promises, 'righteousness exalts a nation'. (Proverbs 14:24)

CHAPTER FIFTEEN

A New Start

Ken returned home near the end of 1994 feeling a mixture of sadness and determination to do something. Naturally, everyone wanted to know what had really happened in Rwanda and particularly in Cyangugu. Experts on Post Traumatic Stress Disorder tell us that the best therapy is to tell your story and allow your memory time to process the events that caused the trauma. Ken was not traumatised, but he did have plenty of opportunity for reflection as he told and re-told what he had seen and heard.

Telling of the past is valuable, but Ken's mind was now turning to the future. He was now fifty eight years old. A love of sport and an active life had kept him healthy, fit and filled with determination to complete the task that God had given him in Rwanda. His home congregations were not neglected; in fact they were blessed as they played their part in the ministry both at home and in Rwanda through prayer, interest and support. Ken had seven years before his official retirement from the post in Rwanda. It was time to make plans!

In 1994 the Bishops of the Anglican Church of Rwanda left the country and went to Kenya, Tanzania and Zaire. The only one who didn't leave was the Bishop of Butare, who died in Nairobi Hospital in December of that year. His successor was studying for a Master's degree in France, and Ken was in England. Four of the ten Rwandan bishops failed to come back to their dioceses when the country was restored to law and order. In 1996, with a little prompting from the Anglican Consultative Council meeting in Panama, the Synod gave notice that if the four failed to return in three months they would be replaced.

Four of them refused to return, so elections took place in each of the four dioceses. Ken, who had been the Assistant Bishop, was elected as Bishop of Cyangugu. It was not a great change as Ken had been running the diocese for two years anyway. But in June of 1997 he was duly 'enthroned' in his new cathedral. He was presented with his Episcopal crook, which he had to buy himself because it was a new diocese without any funds. His bishop's ring was his father's, though he had to have a new stone fitted, because the original was cracked. He brought back a chunk of rock from Rwanda with amethyst in it, which a jeweller in Lewes, Jonathan Swan, cut out and fitted in the ring for him. Amethysts are beautiful semi-precious stones and found in many parts of Africa. His red chimere, white rochet and black scarf were his father's, who had been the last Bishop of the Diocese of Rwanda and Burundi. After him it was divided into two dioceses. By 2001 the two countries between them had fourteen dioceses.

Jill in Mothers Union Uniform with Jane at Ken's enthronement

Ken had kept his father's robes after he died in 1973, never thinking he would actually need them for himself! He used to wear the scarlet chimere on Christmas day at home as Father Christmas, dressing up to give out the family's presents! The ceremonial robes and accoutrements served an important role in Africa. It gave the African congregations and clergy the message that they were valued by the Anglican Church and were worthy of the same attention to ceremonial tradition as anywhere else in the worldwide Anglican communion.

Ken's mind was swimming with plans for the buildings that would be needed for the new Diocese, but the first priority was to assemble a reliable team to work with him. He still needed to spend most of the year in his home parishes in England and also find the time for raising the considerable amount of money that would be needed in Cyangugu.

The story of Bishop Daniel Nduhura is an example of how committed Ken was to his task of training and assisting the men he worked with. Shortly before the genocide, Ken had been consecrated as a Bishop to enable him to assist Bishop Daniel Nduhura to develop the new diocese of Cyangugu, but understandably, after his close call with the Interahamwe, he fled Cyangugu to Bukavu in Congo. After the genocide, Ken visited him and tried to persuade him to return to his ministry but he refused, saying that there was no house, no security and no car. However, Ken had built him a house next to his own, and showed him a photo of it. Because the picture showed a ladder leaning against the house, he said it wasn't finished.

It was clear that he just didn't want to return. Ken offered him the use of his own car – at considerable risk to the vehicle! He still insisted that there was no security. Ken pointed out that there was no security for anyone in Rwanda at that time. He eventually returned to Rwanda in a general repatriation for refugees from Congo but returned to his home town not to Cyangugu. Having fled to Zaire for safety, he was nearly killed by an artillery shell that hit the place where he was staying when that part of eastern Congo descended into a war zone in 1996 with various groups fighting for control of the vast mineral wealth that is in the area, such as diamonds, cobalt, uranium and rare minerals.

Ken had rented a good house for Bishop Daniel before the genocide from an Omani businessman and paid a large rent for two years in advance before Bishop Daniel moved in with his family. When the Bishop fled he packed his things into Ken's Land Rover and a friend's pick-up and crossed into Zaire in the night. The Bishop of Bukavu gave him accommodation and he stayed there for over three years.

Some years later in 1998 the Omani owner of the house discovered that some of his personal belongings were in Bukavu and claimed that the Bishop had taken them. He claimed that if Daniel had not left, his house would not have been stripped bare. This, of course, was not true. The house would have been stripped in any event. Anything Daniel didn't take would certainly have disappeared with the refugees passing through.

The Bishop would only say that he took what could fit in the car and refused to specify what items were taken and how the Omani's items had come to be seen in Bukavu. To save a court case Ken called the *Sous Prefet*, a lawyer from the Court of Appeal and his Diocesan Secretary, to meet with the Omani and the leader of the local Muslim community. Ken negotiated for the whole morning and ended up paying two million Rwanda francs (about £2,000) compensation. Although Bishop Daniel refused to help, it was Ken who had rented the house and signed the contract. So – as on other occasions in his Rwanda ministry – Ken paid up!

Ken urgently needed a Projects Officer to make sure the building work continued while he was not there to drive things along. He was recommended to see if he could recruit Charles Semwaga, who had returned from thirty years as a refugee in Uganda. Ken went to see him at an orphanage in Butare where he was working. He had a burning desire to help the thousands of children left as orphans by the Genocide. The orphanage where he worked was closing down because the children in their care had nearly all been placed into extended families. This is the traditional way that orphans are cared for throughout Africa. The Western passion for building institutionalised orphanages that are expensive to run, and tend to take children out of their own culture, are fine for emergency situations such as war and famine, but are not always the best longer-term solution.

Charles was not keen on coming to a rather dangerous area of Rwanda near the Interahamwe who had fled across the lake to Bukavu in Congo. Ken wanted him because he seemed to have the qualities that he needed for the job. In 1998 he finally agreed to come and they worked very happily together. His wife followed a year later with the children and lived in the house next door to Ken's.

Also high on Ken's list of possible co-workers was Azaria Ndizihiwe, who with his wife Ruth, had the narrow escape from the Interahamwe, when Hutu members of their congregation had courageously intervened to save them. They had crossed the nearby border into Burundi and stayed for a while in a refugee camp – Ruth having given birth to their fourth child in the forest as she fled from the killers!

In September of 1994 he found Azaria and Ruth in Butare, having returned from the refugee camp. He asked them to come back to Cyangugu to help build the new diocese. Ruth, understandably so soon after the trauma of nearly being killed by the Interahamwe, didn't want to return, but Azaria, after some hesitation, courageously agreed. A house was rented for him in the 'Cite', which was the Muslim dominated part of the town. By then Ken had rebuilt a house that he had originally built in 1993, but was reduced to rubble in July 1994.

When he returned home at the end of this trip, he left Azaria's salary in a series of envelopes in a drawer in his house and gave Azaria a key. His instruction was to take an envelope each month during the four months that Ken was back in England. Africans tend to live for today and allow tomorrow to take care of itself. If any special need came up, the temptation for him to take more that one month's salary would be great. As it turned out, Azaria responded to the trust that Ken had put in him and only took one each month.

Ken had decided that if Azaria took only one of those envelopes each month he would promote him and make him an Archdeacon. Ken returned in January to find that the fourth envelope was still in the drawer. Azaria had shown that he was trustworthy and so, at a Sunday service in their temporary church, he knelt in front of him and in the traditional ceremony, promised to obey his Bishop. Ken put an Archdeacon's clerical scarf on him and typed out a certificate.

It was necessary to leave someone in authority, to look after the diocese while he went back to his English parishes and Azaria had shown the key quality that Ken needed, which was integrity. It took some time before Ruth joined her husband in Cyangugu, but eventually she did. As a Mother's Union worker she had to visit the parishes. She found it hard to go to Bweyeye, but when she summoned up the courage, she was overwhelmed by the warmth of her welcome, and she consequently visited there regularly.

Ken's visits continued, enabling him to visit the rural parishes of the Cyangugu diocese regularly. Because of Cyangugu's proximity to the refugee camps across the border in Zaire and its remoteness from the rest of Rwanda, it was still a dangerous area for several years after the Genocide. Gangs of Interahamwe militia were still in the forest through which Ken had to pass every time he travelled between Kigali and Cyangugu. Bored young thugs from the refugee camps became gangs of insurgents and were supported and often directed by sinister leaders from the genocide. During this dangerous time the government provided Ken and anyone else needing to travel that route with a military escort. Three armed soldiers travelled with him in his Land Rover.

The first time Ken picked up his escort, one of the soldiers was a Captain Sabuni, whose grandfather, he discovered, had been trained as a clergyman by Ken's father, Lawrence. Ken asked the officer what he should do if the militia shot at them from the trees as they passed through the forest. He said, *'You stop, my men jump out, and you back off!'*

Ken then asked him 'What would happen if they have laid a land mine in the road?'

He said, *'That's easy. Bishop and soldiers go to heaven together!'*

For the two and a half-hour journey they discussed who goes to heaven and who doesn't! At the end of the journey, Ken gave them all Kinyarwanda Bibles to find 'The Way'.

The church in Cyangugu needed buildings as it does anywhere else, but the church is built first and foremost on godly people. To this end, Ken began the whole process by choosing six catechists from the parishes and bringing them to the town for training. He found an elderly Canon, Yona Bujindiri, who used to be Principal of a Bible College. He lived in Ken's house with the catechists for four months and taught them in preparation for their ordination. After six months, on his next visit Ken ordained them and set them in charge of rural churches.

At the ordination service of the six catechists, Canon Yona Bujindiri, told the congregation his story. He had retired to his home in the east of Rwanda, Gahini, where he lived with his wife, children and grandchildren. On 7th April 1994 the Interahamwe came and forced him to watch while they cut down his wife, grown children and grandchildren. They shouted, as they cut off their hands and ankles, *'You Tutsis are too tall; we'll cut you down to size.'* When they had killed the whole family they slashed the Canon's neck, left him bleeding, and fled as the soldiers of the RPF arrived. The RPF soldiers took him to the hospital where he was treated, and incredibly he survived. He testified that only the Grace of God had enabled him to live in the same house for four months with the six Hutu catechists and teach them. He said God had forgiven him his sins for Christ's sake, so for Christ's sake he forgave those who killed his family. There were many tearful faces in the church that day, when he finished speaking.

*   *   *

Travelling through the Nyungwe Forest in those early days after the genocide, soldiers would sometimes ask for a lift. Ken didn't know whether they were RPF soldiers or those from the former army. None of them had recognisable uniforms and so he was not sure whether to pick them up. Ken asked a Colonel in Cyangugu how he could recognise which side they were on and he gave two indicators. He said the RPF were wearing wellington boots and would look straight at you as you approached. If they were from the old regime, and were being hunted in the forest, they would furtively look round to see who might be watching them. Armed with this advice, he carried on giving lifts to soldiers through the forest. The Bible Society produced hundreds of gospels with camouflage covers and Ken stocked up with these in his Land Rover giving one to every soldier he saw.

If Jill happened to be travelling with Ken on a trip, it was amusing when talking to the soldiers at the many road blocks where Ken would introduce his wife. They sometimes accused him of lying because priests don't have wives! The strong Roman Catholic ethos hadn't yet come to terms with men in clerical collars having wives.

On one journey through the Forest from Cyangugu to Kigali, when Canon Geoffrey Daintree was visiting, the fan belt broke on Ken's Land Rover. Geoffrey, being a bit of a mechanic, said they must stop. But stopping in the forest was strictly forbidden because it was dangerous. They could see the temperature gauge going up, but didn't dare stop. Fortunately, the forest road winds up from Cyangugu at 6,000 feet, to over 8,000 feet in places. So at every downhill section Ken switched the engine off and they coasted downhill with the fan cooling it down enough to get up the next hill, and the next, until eventually they were out of the forest and could finally stop. They tried to improvise using string and some tyre rubber, but it all broke. They managed to limp on to Butare, where they searched the old Arab stores for a belt that fitted the Series III Land Rover and managed to find one before resuming their journey to Kigali.

During these visits, Ken often needed to go from Cyangugu to Kigali, passing through numerous official road blocks, to apply for building permission or change money at the few banks operating at that time. Jill sometimes accompanied Ken on the trips and they stayed at various places in Kigali, always bearing security in mind. During one visit they stayed at the diocesan guest house. Jill was left alone one evening while Ken was out meeting other Bishops when she heard gunfire in the vicinity. This was frightening to say the least. The recent history of the country meant that not only soldiers, but civilians too, often had guns. Add alcohol into the mix and gunfire at night can easily happen. They really needed somewhere safe and affordable to stay.

The surprising solution came on one occasion when they were invited by the American Ambassador to stay at the official residence. This was very secure, though Ken's old Series III short-wheelbase Land Rover looked rather incongruous outside the large and plush ambassador's house. The reason the Ambassador invited Ken to make the house his home when in Kigali, was that his father had been a missionary with his parents in Burundi many years before. Ken and the Ambassador had been at school at the same time, though not at the same school. As a boy, the Ambassador's school was at the Rift Valley Academy in Kijabe, while Ken and his brothers and sisters were at schools in Nairobi. Thus, one of America's ambassador's was able to bless one of God's!

Ken knew that when one of his congregations needed a church to meet in, it was not wise to just to do the whole job and build it for them. They needed to be involved, make their own contribution, and feel some ownership of the project. This also helps to dispel the popular African belief that helpful people from the West have access to a bottomless pit of money! In most areas of life, people value things that have cost them something – even if it is just physical labour.

To this end, Ken and the clergy of the new Diocese of Cyangugu agreed together on how they would divide the effort. Where there was a congregation needing a church, he would buy the land, they would build the church and Ken would provide them with the corrugated iron sheets for the roof – the most costly part of the construction. The members needed to supply the sun dried bricks, window and door frames and shutters etc. and put the whole building together. Working this way, the number of churches in the Diocese began to increase.

In those first few years after the genocide, it was clear to everyone that there would never be security in the southern regions of the country bordering Zaire and around Lake Kivu, while former leaders of the genocide remained in the refugee camps and had access to people willing to cross over the border and cause trouble. The refugees must be repatriated in spite of the efforts of former government militants to keep them in Zaire. Most of the people wanted to go home, and given the chance they would. The issue was settled when the camps themselves came under attack from Zairian rebels who were trying to oust President Mobuto Sese Seko. He had given some help to the refugees and their leaders, probably seeking to enlist their support in any future challenge to his regime in this far distant and mineral-rich area of his country. The refugee camps, probably on the principle that, 'my enemy's friend is my enemy', were coming under attack by rebels from Zaire itself. Jill recalls seeing the refugee tents being set alight as they were all driven out and moved away from the lake. The lake was very quiet as there were no fishing boats allowed, therefore none of the fishermen's normal practice of singing while fishing that would normally be heard. The situation was still far from normal.

Most notable in Ken's long list of people he has travelled to Rwanda with is Dr George Carey, the Archbishop of Canterbury at that time. In May 1995 – only ten months after the RPF had occupied Kigali – the Archbishop decided that he wanted to visit Rwanda and he asked Ken to go to with him to act as his interpreter. He had some meetings at Lambeth Palace with Dr. Carey's staff as they prepared for the trip. The visit was bound to stir a lot of media interest, coming so soon after the genocide, and they had to prepare for a press conference at Kigali airport.

The day of departure arrived and Ken was told to be at Lambeth Palace at 6.30pm for a 7.30pm flight. He couldn't believe that this was the correct timing because they had to drive from Lambeth to Heathrow to check in. He was used to allowing two or three hours at the airport. To allow for a mistake, he arrived at Lambeth Palace much too early and had quite a wait. Ken realised that he needn't have been concerned because at 6.30pm on the dot, the limousine swept up to the steps of the palace with a second car for the staff.

Ken moved towards the second car but was called to the limousine! The Archbishop wanted to go over some of the facts that Ken had supplied as part of his preparation. When they reached Heathrow they went through a VIP entrance that Ken didn't even know existed and the formalities were all dealt with while they were served tea in a comfortable lounge. The three chaplains, Ken and a journalist were in Business Class – not something that Ken was accustomed to. However, later in the flight the steward asked if they would mind moving up to First Class. Ken said he thought they might be able to manage it!

There was a reason for the unexpected upgrade; it was so that when they arrived at Kigali they could all walk out onto the red carpet together. The Bishops and government ministers were lined up to greet His Grace and Mrs Carey as they were ushered into the VIP building for the press conference. The questions were not easy as the main concerns were about the complex issue of justice.

For the Anglican Church in Rwanda this was also a strategic visit, because the Roman Catholic Church had been very close to the government of President Habyarimana and had therefore been associated with the Genocide in the minds of many. The hot issue was, will the Anglican Church be pressing for justice concerning the perpetrators of the genocide? From the press conference at the airport to questions on the last day, this was the major concern.

They were taken to the Mille Collines Hotel, which was their base for the week. Throughout the visit Ken had to keep close to the Archbishop so he could interpret, and identify each person. In the UN helicopter, which flew them to a number of centres, His Grace had a notepad on which he wrote questions and passed to Ken for an answer.

At the University hospital in Butare, the Dean of the Faculty of Medicine gave them a sad account of the Interahamwe coming in to finish off the wounded Tutsis, and how Hutu nurses and doctors turned on their colleagues and killed Tutsi doctors and nurses.

They were taken to a large Catholic church where thousands had been killed. When the killings began people rushed to the churches for sanctuary. In the case of the church they were visiting, the priest had been ordered to separate the Tutsis and bring them out. He refused, saying that they were all members of the same Church. The priest and the whole congregation were then brutally murdered whether Tutsi or Hutu. Just a year after the killings the bodies still lay where they had fallen and there was blood on the walls and on the Communion Table. It was a truly shocking sight that no one who witnessed it will ever forget.

While Archbishop Carey was in one particular meeting with a government minister, Ken was waiting with the Archbishop's wife, Eileen. Later, the Archbishop asked him if Jill ever travelled to Rwanda with him. The question may have been prompted by the Archbishop's wife. Ken told the Archbishop that they usually couldn't afford the air tickets for Jill. He then stated he would pay for Jill to accompany Ken once a year until he was sixty five and had to retire. He also asked why he spent most of his time in the UK when the Rwandans needed him so much. Ken told him it was because the parish still paid his stipend. Archbishop Carey then replied that if it enabled him to spend more time in Africa he would arrange a grant for him of £4,000 a year. He would also provide him with a letter which he could forward to churches he worked with, to suggest they might like to help provide an income for them.

True to his word, the Archbishop did everything he had suggested and Ken stopped receiving the stipend from Chichester Diocese. The £4,000 went to the Diocesan Board of Finance, which qualified him for a pension at sixty five. A number of churches granted contributions from 1995 until his retirement in 2001. Ken and Jill were very impressed and grateful to Dr Carey, both for his kindness and his recognition of the importance of what God was calling Ken to do in the wounded country of Rwanda. After 2001, when Ken reached the retirement age of sixty five, the huge blessing of having a clergy pension deposited into his bank every month caused Ken and Jill to want to sing hymns of praise! Financially, things had never been easy for them.

The final meeting of the Archbishop's visit was in the 60,000 seat football stadium, called the Amahoro (peace) stadium. Ken was shown to a seat between Dr George and Mrs Eileen Carey. Next to the Archbishop was the Vice President, Major General Paul Kagame and next to Mrs Carey was the President (Speaker) of the National Assembly. Ken had to interpret all the speeches, which were in Kinyarwanda, in a voice loud enough for both the Carey's to hear. It was a bit embarrassing that the Vice President and Speaker could hear also!

During the programme a number of people welcomed the chief guest and thanked him for coming. Then the Archbishop's turn came. Before he went to the microphone, he quickly said to Ken 'I see I am down to speak again later, write me a speech!' He made the major set speech, which he had worked on with Ken earlier. He didn't have to interpret into the local vernacular Kinyarwanda as one of the Rwandan bishops was able to do this.

When it came to his second speech he delivered everything that Ken had written, but adding a bit of his own, which was brilliant. He stated he had been sitting in the football stadium next to General Kagame. Both were keen football supporters. The following Saturday he would be watching the FA Cup Final in Wembley Stadium, London. He commentated that he would be in the royal box and the TV cameras would be focused on him. He announced that he would be waving enthusiastically and the people in England would assume he was cheering for his team, when actually he would be 'waving to you in Rwanda to cheer you on!' The applause was deafening!

In 1995, Ken, having had experience of dairy farming in his background, wondered if there was something he could do to help the community replace the many cattle that were slaughtered in 1994. He approached the local authorities and discussed the issue. They asked if he would restore a veterinary dispensary which had been destroyed. More property was destroyed and more people were killed in Cyangugu in the genocide, than anywhere else in Rwanda. In the Cyangugu Diocese the Genocide killed most of the Tutsi population in the area.

Ken and his team agreed to restore and run the veterinary dispensary. They rebuilt it and employed two local vets, one to run the dispensary and one to treat sick animals in the area. They built cow stalls, both brick and wooden ones for demonstrations. Bricks were more expensive to build with because it required expensive cement. He bought two cross-bred cows and six Friesians. Next came a chicken house and Ken bought a hundred and fifty chicks, which then produced eggs regularly. As calves were born they were sold to local people who could build suitable accommodation as demonstrated. The result of this work and investment meant that they were able to supply milk, eggs, calves and treatment.

With the return of two million refugees in 1997, the government began a process of creating 'villages' to house those who had no home. Some just didn't want to return to the neighbourhoods where they had either assisted the genocide, or stood silently by. This 'villagisation' involved building simple houses of poles and mud in rows, or in groups. The work was done largely by the United Nations High Commission for Refugees (UNHCR). In Cyangugu the hill called Mont Cyangugu, originally designated for permanent brick houses, was divided in two, separated by three court buildings. The 'Court of First Instance' at the top of the hill was formerly the local headquarters of the MRND, the political party of the former government.

The Appeal Court was the only other building on the hill. Two of these buildings were dealing with prisoners accused of Genocide. The third was the police court which had been moved from its site near the border and dealt with everyday cases of theft and debts. Soldiers guarding that court would often come down to Ken's house for a chat and a cool bottle of Fanta to while away the time and, presumably, to check out what everyone was getting up to as it was still very insecure there on the border with Zaire.

One side of the hill is now covered with two hundred and fifty village-type houses, with mainly mud walls and iron roofs supplied by UNHCR. Locally it is known collectively as 'Mudugudu'.

On the other side of Mont Cyangugu the Prefecture gave the diocese a building plot for staff houses. Ken built five of the scheduled nine. Two of these and the kindergarten, were built by prisoners from the local prison. It was government policy to give those awaiting trial a chance to see the outside world, get some exercise and earn some cash for their families. The quality of their work depended on the way they were treated.

Ken's Projects Co-ordinator, Charles Semwaga, worked with them, supplying all the material and directing operations. The Building Inspector later commented that the houses and the school were very strongly built. A good example of the way Rwandans are coping with the aftermath of the Genocide was the way this Projects Co-ordinator treated the prisoners. Charles, a Tutsi, had seen many of his family killed in the Genocide. He was now working with Hutu prisoners all accused of involvement in the killings. It wasn't just the President and his government who knew that the only way forward for Rwanda was for all the ethnic groups to be united together under the one banner of being Rwandan, the people were beginning to see the vision too.

Evangelist Charles Semwaga

CHAPTER SIXTEEN

A Millennium Project

In the immediate aftermath of the genocide, uppermost in Ken's mind when he was visiting Cyangugu, was finding a team to work with, restoring damaged properties, and always being aware of the difficult security situation in that part of Rwanda. Then as things normalised as far as they could at that time, Ken began to think and plan for the years ahead leading to the new millennium, and his own retirement the following year. The vision that crystallised in his mind was to build the Cyangugu diocese into a thriving community serving all the people that lived there and administered by a well trained team of clergy. He began to think of it as a project to mark Christ's 2000th birthday.

The approach of the millennium somehow gave a greater meaning to what he was planning. He wasn't doing anything for himself or building some little empire in his own name, he was building God's kingdom in that part of Africa. He wanted it to be for the glory of Christ. He had the vision and now he needed a plan to translate that into a reality. It would be the 'MILLENNIUM PROJECT', to mark this special point in history.

Throughout 1999 the imminent arrival of the new millennium was a constant theme of the media in most parts of the world; especially in the West. A multitude of events were being planned to mark the great occasion. Not least in the minds of government and business alike was the 'Millennium Bug'. Woe to anyone, business, government or nation that did not plan for the time when masses of computer controlled systems would all break down at the stroke of midnight, and civilisation as we know it would come to an end if we didn't re-programme the computers' clocks to take account of the first two digits of the date changing from '19..' to '20..' – a fact that the makers of all computers and everything controlled by computers seemed, amazingly, to have overlooked!

People stocked up on foodstuffs and bottled water to help them to survive after the 'Bug' had reduced western civilisation to chaos. Armies of technicians were trained to adjust the computer systems of governments, banks, stores, London Underground, air traffic controllers and all strategic computers. Many night flights for that date were cancelled. As the fateful midnight arrived, millions of people watched the celebrations on television with one eye while keeping the other on their computer. In the event, nothing happened and it proved to be the biggest false alarm in the history of the planet! Everyone breathed a somewhat embarrassed sigh of relief.

Grandpa enjoying his grandchild

Ken however, was preparing for the Millennium in a different and more meaningful way. Away with those pedantic people who quibbled over the actual date, the concept was inspiring. Ken was an enthusiastic publicist for the historic changes for good that were taking place in Rwanda since the government, led by Paul Kigame had come to power in 1994. The Millennium Dome in East London reminded him of Matthew 23:37 '...*how often I have longed to gather your children together, as a hen gathers her chicks under her wings.*' The God of love had His hand over the land of Rwanda, and under this 'dome' the people would be dealing with the hurts and the fears engendered by the terrible events that had taken place and planning for a better future. This may seem idealistic to some, but Rwanda was a country desperately in need of ideals at that time. This small crowded African nation would be united metaphorically under one national 'Dome'. It was a great vision and it had come from God.

*   *   *

In the years between 1995 and the Millennium, God led Ken to meet people and receive invitations to places that would enable the plan to become a reality. In 1997 an international SOMA (Sharing Of Ministries Abroad) team came to Rwanda and sent groups to every one of the nine Anglican dioceses. The group that came to Cyangugu included two New Zealanders, one a 'Pakeha' (white), the other a Maori. Their mission was very popular with the Rwandan Christians and they soon had people falling backwards in 'Toronto blessing' style. The Maori Archdeacon Bert Karaka, was very impressed with Cyangugu, with the lake and the forest, and so touched by the stories of Genocide, that he decided to ask his Bishop to invite Ken to New Zealand to tell the amazing story of Rwanda and its recovery.

In February 1997 the plan materialised. Bert, with the help of the Anglican Church of New Zealand and CMS (NZ), bought return tickets for Ken and Jill to fly to New Zealand for a three week speaking tour of the North and South Islands. They were met by Bert Karaka on their arrival and he took them to a number of meetings with groups of Maori. In the cultural manner of the Maori, Jill and the leader's wife processed into the meeting from the entrance, Bert and Ken would follow. A Maori then made a speech in his own language and the group then sang in the beautiful harmony for which the Maori are famous. Bert would then respond, and then Ken, to the delight of his audience, had to sing in Kinyarwanda! The tour was well prepared and Ken spoke at thirty-nine meetings. The journeys by car gave him time to prepare while Jill enjoyed the sightseeing.

During the meetings Ken showed a series of colour acetates on an overhead projector (OHP) giving background information on Rwanda, an update on the country and progress in building the new diocese of Cyangugu. OHP acetates shown on a big screen proved to be a useful means of illustrating the subject in large churches or halls as well as in smaller home meetings. There was a different audience at each meeting and so the same set of pictures and stories could be repeated at all the venues. This saved him the need to spend a lot of time in preparing visual aids for meetings; time that would be difficult to find given the number of meetings and the travelling in between.

By the third week Jill remarked that she could easily have given the talk herself. She had the job of changing the acetates and knew what was going to be said next, even the jokes! As there was an Anglican Primates' Conference on at the time, the crack about the thirteen primates in Rwanda's Nyungwe Forest went down well with the largely Anglican audiences!

The stories people wanted to hear most were related to the reconciliation. How the Tutsi and Hutu were now able to live together after the events of 1994. Particularly the account of the Hutu ordination candidates and their Tutsi teacher, whose family were all killed, was of great interest. The Tutsi Projects Co-ordinator, Charles, using two hundred Hutu prisoners, all accused of genocide, was also an encouragement to everyone. Charles had many members of his family killed. In African culture, it was his duty to try to care for the family's children left orphaned. By God's grace, he bore no apparent bitterness towards them. The account of how he worked with the prisoners and talked to them civilly, which caused them to work harder for him, was inspiring. The accounts of the Genocide moved Bert Karaka deeply. Being in a leadership role in an ethnic minority community must have made the stories all the more poignant.

New Zealand is a beautiful land, and Ken and Jill had the opportunity to see a number of the many attractive features as they visited various parts of the country. They saw the Kauri trees on the west coast, which were growing when Christ was on earth. They enjoyed the coach trip along the ninety mile beach seeing people skiing down the sand dunes on sledges, and the hurricane at Cape Reinga where the two oceans met and the war canoe in the Bay of Islands.

An extraordinary experience at Queenstown was the Jet Ski boat ride down the canyon, where the driver heads at great speed towards the canyon wall. Ken asked the boat driver if he ever hit the rock walls as he drove at such speeds and he replied 'Not often!' Sadly, some months after their visit there was a fatal accident when one of the drivers got it wrong. The hot springs and their pools were also fun.

By the end of this memorable trip Ken and Jill had slept in no fewer than nineteen different beds!

*   *   *

The Millennium Project was given a further boost when Ken attended the Thirteenth Lambeth Conference (which occurs every ten years) in 1998, where seven hundred and forty nine Bishops and their spouses of the Worldwide Anglican Communion had gathered. It was presided over by Archbishop George Carey. The Bishops were divided into groups of about twelve, to study the book of 1 Corinthians. In Ken's group were Bishops from Sudan, Nigeria and one David Bane, a newly consecrated bishop whose diocese was Southern Virginia, USA. Ken and David quickly found a rapport with each other. Both had interesting stories to tell and they had good fellowship swapping accounts of how God had led them over the years.

David Bane had been in the US Air Force and had come out with a serious alcohol problem. His wife and family left him because he was dangerous when drunk, being a big fellow! In the depths of despair he was led to know Jesus Christ, who totally changed his life, leading eventually to ordination and the episcopate. They met together with two other friends at the final barbecue at the Canterbury University Campus, where the conference was held.

One of David's friends was David Jones, Suffragan Bishop of Virginia. Another was Ken Price, Suffragan Bishop of Southern Ohio. Ken and Jill had previously met Ken Price in New Zealand the year before. The three American bishops invited Ken to be the keynote speaker at their Diocesan Conventions. When they returned to the States they put together a programme, then the invitation came for both to fly to Washington. The diocese of Virginia was the first stop on their itinerary.

David Jones arranged accommodation for them in what Ken and Jill considered to be a luxury hotel, where the convention was being held. They enjoyed three very comfortable days with all expenses paid by the diocese! Ken illustrated his speech with OHP coloured photos on a large screen for the two hundred delegates. At the end of the talk he presented his Millennium Project for Cyangugu. In the subsequent Virginia Diocesan meeting on finances, they granted Ken $25,000 for the project.

From that hotel they were taken to another, equally as grand in Richmond, Virginia, where Ken was to preach at St James's Parish Church on the Sunday. This church had been burnt down and they had built a wonderful new one with the insurance, incorporating the Tiffany windows salvaged from the wreckage. It had meeting rooms, bathrooms and a multi-storey car park. They were taken to visit a number of groups where he was asked to talk about Rwanda, before being driven to Norfolk, in the Diocese of Southern Virginia.

Here they stayed in the beautiful riverside home of Bishop David Bane and his wife Alice, within site of the big naval port of Norfolk. This Diocesan Convention, in a hotel in Renton, Virginia, was David's first, so he was rather apprehensive and therefore glad to have a little encouragement from his English guest. However, he coped very well and the meetings went smoothly. Again Ken used his OHP acetates on a large screen, which gave the delegates an insight into his work and interest in his Millennium Project.

They enjoyed a few restful days back in Norfolk before flying to Columbus, Ohio for their third diocesan visit. Ken spoke at a number of churches including a 'black church'. Having grown up in 'black Africa' he was struck by the fact that he only saw one man with a black (in fact, dark brown) skin. All the congregation were really light brown, except a few white people who worshipped there. Such is the mixed genetic heritage of the 'African Americans'.

Ken and Jill were shown round the town by the Mayor of Columbus who presented Ken with a very smart book about the town. He spoke at a clergy meeting and illustrated it with the inevitable acetates. At the end of the meeting a Rector asked how much a primary school would cost in Rwanda. Ken replied '$37,500'. He replied *'You've got it.'* implying that he would raise that money.

Ken kept in touch with him over the years, but never received the money! They were taken from Columbus to Cincinnati, to another smart hotel. He preached in the cathedral which had just had six million dollars spent on it. They were shown round the City Hall which had also been restored for thirteen million dollars. The big meeting was in the Proctor Camp which had been set up with millions more dollars from the Proctor Foundation, from which Ken received forty thousand dollars for the Millennium Project. The tour was turning out to be very strategic in enabling the Millennium Project to become a reality.

Altogether Ken and Jill had three very interesting weeks in that part of the USA. A year later, David and Alice Bane visited Cyangugu, their first visit to Africa. Ken compiled a programme for them in the diocese, where David shared in one ordination and one confirmation. He probably confirmed more people in that one parish than he would all through his ministry in Southern Virginia! Ken remembers taking his party in two Land Rovers to visit a parish in the natural forest of Nyungwe. As they came to yet another very rickety bridge David crossed himself and prayed 'Our Father who art in heaven…' But before he could pray any further they were safely over the bridge so everyone said 'AMEN!'

After a week in the diocese Ken took them to the north of Rwanda where they travelled to see Rwanda's famous gorillas. They finally flew to a safari park in Kenya which Ken had arranged with an old school friend of his, Anthony Church. David and Alice returned to the United States feeling very excited about Africa!

Early in 1998, the General Secretary of the Mid Africa Ministry (formerly Ruanda Mission, CMS), asked if Ken would be interested to meet a married couple from San Diego who had offered themselves as volunteer missionaries. He flew to their home to visit them and assess if they would fit into the set-up in Cyangugu. He was met at San Diego airport and driven straight to a parish church in an oasis of Yuma in the Arizona desert. He was accommodated with the Rector, Tom Phillips, whose wife was English. Without time to catch his breath or overcome jet-lag, Ken preached in his church twice the next day.

The following day, Tom and his wife took him to a restaurant way out in the desert, where he was treated to a fabulous meal, before being driven back to San Diego. While there, Ken flew to Seattle to see if he could have an interview with Bill Gates! So many amazing things had happened for Ken in the USA that he was beginning to think anything was possible in this very friendly land. He wanted to tell the richest man in the world about his project to equip a secondary school in Rwanda with computers.

There wasn't much time available before his return flight, but Ken managed to get through to an assistant of Mr Gates, called Ruby, who told him to fill in an application form for a grant. She told him that most of his charity money went to projects in Washington State, but remarked it was worth trying. Still aiming high, Ken said he really wanted to talk to Bill Gates personally, but she informed him that he wasn't there. Of course, she could easily say that because the Microsoft complex is like a small town and he could be in any of the buildings and be 'not here.' Ken flew back to San Diego without any donations for his schools' computer needs.

Anyone in the field of raising funds will be aware that it is relationships that matter.

God had led Ken to meet some good men whose dioceses were in the famously generous United States. Ken hoped to convince his audiences that building an Anglican Diocese in Rwanda was a cause worthy of their support. This proved to be the case and the visits were indeed fruitful. At the end of the visit, the diocese of Cyangugu benefited by over $65,000. Ken's mind went into overdrive planning the most strategic way to use the funds.

CHAPTER SEVENTEEN

A Vision Fulfilled

If the Millennium Plan was to become a reality, featuring the necessary infrastructure for a successful diocese in the remote southern part of Rwanda and be more or less complete by the 2000th birthday of Christ, it was going to require money, and lots of it! From September 1994 Ken raised further funds in UK and in USA and continued his building programme.

The diocesan staff team in Cyangugu consisted of Anglophone, Francophone returnees as well as those who never left Rwanda. It was a mixture of Hutu and Tutsi who worked very happily together. Working alongside each other in the diocesan offices helped them to build team camaraderie as they all worked closely together and prayed together daily in the chapel.

In 1998 the then Vice President, Paul Kagame, (later the President of Rwanda), agreed to come to Cyangugu and officially open the dispensary, farm, secondary school and phase one of the guest house. He tried to make this type of visit around the country as often as his busy schedule would allow because he was pleased to see development projects which raised the standard of living of the people and he wanted to encourage them. In his speech he thanked Ken and his team for what they had built in Cyangugu and even stated he would give him a Friesian cow from his own herd as a sign of thanks. The speech was in Kinyarwanda, but he turned to Jill and said in English, *'A Friesian cow from my own herd.'* Jill had been delayed with shingles on her face, but thanks to Captain and Mrs Baller, Jill's sister, arrived in their Land Rover in time for the opening.

To be given a cow is a traditional sign of friendship in Rwandan culture, and because this visit was broadcast on national radio and television it opened a number of important doors. For instance, Ken was called to the Ministry of the Interior and ushered into the minister's office. The minister said he had heard what he had done in Cyangugu and wanted to express his thanks personally. He said he would also like to do something practical to express his thanks. Ken's years in Africa had taught him a thing or two about politicians. When they did something for you, it often meant that one day they may ask you to return a favour or support them in some way. It was important that Ken and the church he represented were not identified with any political party or government.

Ken asked the minister if he could first tell him a story, to which he agreed. He quoted an illustration given by the Archbishop of Kenya at the funeral of the Bishop of Butare in 1994. He had said: 'The church should treat the government like fire.'

Ken expanded on the Archbishop's advice: 'If you get too close you burn, if you get too far away you freeze. You should stand near enough to know what the government was planning and doing, so that if there were events being planned like the Genocide, you could speak out. If you were too close to the government you would be unable to speak out. If you were too far away you would never know what was being planned.' One of the accusations of the Church in 1994 was that the leaders were very close to the government and must have known what was being planned at least two years before the Genocide started, and yet no word of it reached the ears of the Church outside the country.

Having said his piece about the Archbishop's sermon, Ken said to the minister 'If I see this government treating people badly or favouring one group over another, I want to be free to speak out and not to be gagged by gifts.' The minister agreed that that was fair enough and a good principle. Having accepted Ken's proviso, the minister still wanted to do something to help him with his work. Cows may be a sign of friendship, but the minister offered Ken something far more useful; he said he would give him Permanent Residence and a Rwandan Diplomatic passport.

Ken thanked him and, thinking quickly, asked if he could make one request, *'Could I have the same for my wife too?'* to which he agreed! Anyone who travels regularly to African countries will be very familiar with the tiresome wait in long queues at immigration to pay for entry visas, and glancing across enviously at the one or two people in the line marked 'Diplomatic Passports Only', will appreciate just what a blessing this was.

One night around midnight, Ken had just gone to bed, when his watchman knocked on his bedroom door to tell him that there were soldiers at the gate. Ken arose and put on his dressing gown and went out to find the local Colonel, escorted as usual by ten soldiers. He came in and asked when Ken was going to England. He gave him the date, and the Colonel then asked to borrow his telephone.' He rang the Vice President and told him when Ken was due to leave the country. They chatted a bit then the Colonel and ten soldiers departed.

Two days before Ken flew home, he was told to go to the farm. A lorry arrived with a beautiful Friesian heifer in-calf. This heifer's mother, on the General's farm, was giving forty litres of milk a day. Ken's farm workers looked after the donated cow as best they could, but they never achieved forty litres. With improved water supply and implementing a zero grazing programme, the milk yield later increased. Her first two calves were bulls, one of which was sold. The other had to be put down as the farm had already bought a Friesian bull from another farmer. There was no water supply laid on, so the herdsmen had the exhausting task of carrying it up the steep hill from the spring at the bottom. They bought an old tank and one of Ken's guests, Ian Betts, managed to put up some guttering to catch the rainwater off the corrugated iron roof. They later repaired another brick tank taking water from another roof. This gives enough water for the cattle in the rainy season, which eased the herdsmen's burdens at that time of the year.

In 1999 Ken accepted an invitation to be the key note speaker at the Diocesan Convention of the Diocese of the Rio Grande in New Mexico, USA and Jill accompanied him. After the convention, they flew from there to Cost Rica in Central America, to spend a few days with their daughter Sue, her husband Ken, and their two grandchildren Joshua and Hannah. They had no telephone in the young peoples' training camp where they worked, so Ken went to a hotel where there was a phone and called their son to confirm some arrangements for their return.

The news that Ken heard from home was deeply shocking and raised serious problems for him and his home parish. The Rev Nigel Holmes and his wife Anne, both of whose parents had worked in Rwanda, had been looking after the two parishes for eight weeks and had already made a good impression. They visited the homes, led Bible studies and services together and were greatly appreciated by everyone.

Early one morning, Nigel went running as normal, but didn't come back to bring his wife her morning tea. Nigel had collapsed and died! His body was found slumped against a telephone box in Battle. Ken and Jill flew back immediately to comfort Anne and make preparations for the funeral. Ken also had to decide what to do about the parishes. He had become more and more involved in the Diocese of Cyangugu and couldn't leave his Millennium Project without leadership just as the plan was about to come to the end of its present phase, leading up to the end of the year.

The funeral was a triumphant occasion when family and friends witnessed to the strong faith and many gifts of this humble man of God. Children and grandchildren revealed aspects of his full life of sport, music and love of nature. Now Ken had to decide what to do about the parish work. Nigel and Anne had offered to 'hold the fort' until he was sixty five and had to retire from the diocese in Rwanda, as stated in the constitution of the Rwanda Province.

It was not easy to find an honorary curate at such short notice and there were only eighteen months left before his retirement. As a solution Ken decided to create a Ministry Team, with Anne as Administrator and two retired clergy, Malcolm Bury and Bill Maxwell, helping with the services. Once again, Ken had the support of those who knew of his Rwandan ministry. His parishes supported the team idea and he was able to complete his Millennium plan in Cyangugu. The Diocese of Chichester also approved of the Ministry Team idea. Ken returned to the work in Africa confident that the parishes were in good hands.

Through all the years of ministry in Rwanda, Jill played her part with diligence and courage. As a young woman, her plan was to be a missionary in East Africa. When she had the encounter with MS and everything changed, she may have thought that her ambition to make a contribution to building God's kingdom in Africa had passed her by. However, in God's plan, this was certainly not the case!

Apart from her opportunities to travel with Ken, while he was in Rwanda creating the new diocese, Jill would be at home in Battle, keeping in touch with the two parishes of Ashburnham and Penhurst, where Ken was still the Incumbent. She visited many of the people in the two villages and of course attended the services on Sundays. She organised many fund raising activities and was greatly supported by the clergy of the Deanery of Battle and Bexhill who promised to pray for Ken and Jill in their ministry and development work.

While Ken was in Africa, Jill often came under spiritual attack, with things going wrong in the house. She says their neighbours had come to expect that when Ken was away all sorts of disasters would happen. Deep snow higher than the hedges one year, a hurricane bringing down hundreds of trees and scores of telephone and electricity cables in 1987 and the car giving trouble another time. There was even a

At Rosewood together

phone call once from someone in a nearby town saying how sorry they were to hear that Ken and his visitors had been kidnapped in Rwanda! He had seen it on the Internet posted by someone in Kansas. Ken had never been kidnapped and has no idea where the rumour came from.

*   *   *

The time eventually arrived for Ken to hand over the diocese of Cyangugu to his successor. Only seven years after its inception it was well equipped to face the future. He was able to hand over a diocese, which although in the remotest part of Rwanda, had fifty rural churches served by seventeen clergy. It also had twelve good staff houses, each with water and electricity and five with telephones and a Bishop's office with six staff offices. On the farming side there was livestock, a demonstration farm and a dispensary. Larger additions included an assembly hall able to hold seven hundred, and an income generating guest house with fifty two beds on the picturesque shores of Lake Kivu, which Ken named 'Peace Guest House. To improve the education in the area Ken built two secondary schools and four primary schools. The last school to be built before Ken retired was a technical school, with money raised by a LOAF (an inter-church group in Hastings) sponsored walk, teaching carpentry, brickwork, sewing and car mechanics. Ken was a clergyman, but that only tells half of his story. Before he was ever ordained, he was a farmer and a builder and he never lost the love of getting his hands dirty, or of the smells of the farm! All of these were completed without leaving any debt. *'How good is the God we adore?'*

The fundraising provision was extremely important to the future of the projects. There are many examples of fine ministries and aid projects established in Africa by good people, both missionaries and NGOs with Western resources, which collapsed once the Westerners returned home or retired. They proved to be unsustainable without the continued flow of Western money and expertise, or trustworthy men and women to lead the project. The way Ken had set up the whole Cyangugu diocese meant it had a good chance of defying this trend, become self-supporting and continuing to thrive.

In 1999 the local Committee of Genocide Survivors asked Ken to build a dispensary and a nursery school for their children aged four to six; normal schooling starts at age seven in Rwanda. They wanted the teaching to be in English and have a Christian ethos. Ken could see the value of this early Christian influence on the children and the flying start to their education. It would mean they acquired an early grasp of English. French was now definitely out of favour in Rwanda; English was the order of the day. The land for these buildings was given to the church by the Prefecture, or Local Government. But, as with all good ideas, Ken had to set about finding the funds to build a decent school. As with all fundraising, the first step was prayer.

The answer came when Ken and Jill were attending a conference for clergy at the Hayes Conference Centre in Swanwick, Derbyshire. They took the opportunity to talk about this request. The vicar of St Matthew's Church in Cheltenham announced he would make it the subject of the Christmas collections. The generous parishioners of St. Matthew's rose to the challenge and the result was a cheque for thirteen thousand pounds. The nursery school could now be built. This type of charitable giving is always the most efficient. One hundred percent of the money given goes to the project and nothing is deducted.

Ken and the Rwandan project manager Charles Semwaga, employed prisoners from the local prison, all accused of participation in the genocide, to do the building. Ken paid them an agreed sum, which went to their account for their families. In addition to helping the prisoners' families, it was also excellent rehabilitation for the men. The school was built with three nursery classrooms for children under the school age of seven, followed by six Primary classrooms. Charles and Juliet found Christian teachers who spoke English, and the school was opened with the approval of the government authorities.

Having provided a good start to the education of the children, the question then arose of how they could continue to be educated in English. The nearest English medium boarding school was two hundred miles away in Kigali; there was none in the Western region of Rwanda. Ken and Jill had only one answer to a need such as this; if they needed a secondary school, then one must be built!

He had bought a plot of land just below that primary school three years previously, but had no money to build on it at that time. The rules of the Rwanda government are that land scheduled for building must be used within two or three years or it will be given or sold to someone else. They don't want to see prime land left unused. Four of the eighteen plots originally purchased from the local authority had already been lost, and had been sold on for others to use. It took Ken days of negotiating, to get it back, writing letters and eventually paying over the odds in compensation to the four people who had purchased those plots of land.

There was an additional benefit to the method Ken used for building; it was deliberately not ultra-modern. No mechanical diggers or other machines, just manual labour. Ken used people – lots of them. They dug the foundations and moved hundreds of tons of soil with hoes and shovels. Each person he employed had several dependants who will look to him or her for help. Those dependents would also benefit from the salaries paid to the builders. The large majority of the population do not have paid labour and have to make a living off their land.

To begin raising the money, Ken went to the Channel Island of Jersey, whose Overseas Aid Committee (as it was called then) had funded a lot of his projects in the 1980s. He met with some members of the Commission and outlined the project and, to Ken's delight, they agreed to sponsor it, subject to it going through an agency they had dealt with before. The Christian Aid office in Kigali agreed to oversee it and it was proposed to the Aid Commission in Jersey, who then replied that they were not able to fund it!

Ken and Jill wrote about this in their newsletter of December 2008 with the heading *'Bad News at Christmas'*. This brought a remarkable response and the £169,000 needed was found, and in the bank account within the year. Part of that sum did, in the end come from the Overseas Aid Commission in Jersey. They were kind enough to give Ken an opportunity to appeal their original decision. Ken sat with the whole Commission at the States building and outlined the project again, with photographs and drawings of what was planned, as he emphasised the need. They explained that their offer had not been a definite offer because it had never been put in writing. However, they agreed to fund it to the tune of £58,994.

The school was duly completed and named 'St Matthews College, Cyangugu'. It initially had three classrooms, a laboratory and a library/computer room with thirteen laptop computers using Microsoft XP. Given the African's passion for education, it is difficult to imagine anything better than these schools to lift the spirits of the local people and give them hope for the future. It also powerfully witnessed that the Gospel of Jesus Christ demonstrates the love of God in these very practical ways.

CHAPTER EIGHTEEN

A New Rwanda

The post-Genocide government of Rwanda is working hard at encouraging all its citizens to take pride in being Rwandans. In every community, institution and school, Hutu and Tutsi are together. Of course it is to be expected that there are residual hurts and fears. There are still accusations and suspicions, and these must be dealt with by the administration and the courts. Under the 'dome' all this is being done – some would say 'not perfectly' – but without doubt more effectively than anyone dared to expect. Rwanda is now a peaceful place in which to live. Foreign aid and economic development have flowed confidently into the country. The new constitution does not allow the political parties to be ethnically based or to promote their cause on the basis of ethnicity.

One of the recommendations of the Arusha Accords was that the Rwandan government should set up a 'National Unity and Reconciliation Commission' (NURC). The previous government didn't implement this because they had already planned the genocide. Once the genocide was over and the new government took charge, they realised that the need for this was then even greater. The Government of National Unity set up the NURC in March 1999, and it is now a national institution, provided for in the new National Constitution adopted by Rwandans in June 2003. Item six of the NURC's mission statement reads: *'Denouncing and fighting against acts, writings and utterances which are intended to promote any kind of discrimination, intolerance or xenophobia.'*

The international community, having failed Rwanda so badly in 1994, are now perhaps seeking to atone for their previous inaction by stepping up to assist Rwanda and encourage the national unity efforts. Hopefully, they are taking note that genuine reconciliation is taking place in Rwanda. The churches and the NURC are conducting seminars on unity and reconciliation in every part of the country. With so many of the people in Rwanda attending church, this is an effective means of getting the message out and bringing about a new way of thinking in the minds of the population. The success of their work can be judged by the remarkable phenomenon of the Hutu people, whose extremists planned and executed the horrors of the genocide, and the Tutsi, whose families and friends were massacred, living and working together throughout the land. It is hard to think of a comparable process anywhere else in the world.

The radio, which had been a powerful force for evil before and during the Genocide, is now being used for good. Radio communicators promote unity instead of ethnic violence and hatred and there is a growing sense of being one nation. It is safe to travel to any part of the country, for Rwandans and ex-patriots, remarkable so soon after the horrors of 1994.

Numerous accounts of the Rwanda Genocide have been written in books, magazines, Internet postings and several films have been made. Some are impartial, but some are blatantly biased and unreliable. This biography does not attempt to describe the events of 1994 in detail, but rather to describe an important part of the background and context of Ken Barham's ministry and his association with this part of Africa throughout most of his life. For those wanting a fuller account of the genocide and how it came about, Ken recommends Philip Gourevitch's compelling book titled *'We wish to inform you that tomorrow we will be killed with our families.'*

After reading Gourevitch's book, Ken could only echo the statement that Claire Short, (a British former Minister for Overseas Development), wrote in the Daily Telegraph, *'Let's not fail victims of genocide again.'*

Gourevitch writes (p149), *'On December 11, 1946, the General Assembly of the United Nations declared genocide a crime under international law. On December 9 1948, the General Assembly went further, adopting Resolution Z60A (III), the Convention of the Prevention and Punishment of the Crime of Genocide, which obliged "Contracting Parties" to undertake to prevent and punish acts committed with intent to destroy, in whole or in part, a national, ethnical, racial or religious group'.*

Gourevitch goes on to suggest a reason for the apparent indifference the world displayed to the Rwandan Genocide: *'Rwanda is landlocked and dirt-poor. As far as the political, military and economic interests of the world's powers go, it might as well be Mars. In fact, Mars is probably of greater strategic concern. But Rwanda suffered genocide, and the world's powers left Rwanda to it'.*

Gourevitch's account of the refugee camps (p269), triggered painful memories for Ken and Jill. They had looked at camps across Lake Kivu from their Cyangugu house and saw large convoys of huge UNHCR food trucks rolling right past their church door and over the bridge to the Zaire camps. The hungry people in Rwanda watched the refugees being fed in the camps, which were dominated by the perpetrators of the genocide.

Rwanda was peaceful enough to hold presidential elections in 2003 and again on August 9th 2010 which were judged by the head of the Commonwealth Observer Group to be 'free and fair.' There were a few incidents of violence before the elections which are being vigorously investigated and the strict laws will be implemented with the culprits.

The country is also now cleaner than most African countries. The streets in Kigali are cleaned daily and there are no plastic bags, which used to litter the ditches and trees. Now they are totally forbidden in the country. This is not a minor measure. It helps to create a higher national self-esteem and raises the aspirations of the population.

*　　　*　　　*

Mary Izajiriza

The remarkable story of Mary Izajiriza is not unique in post-Genocide Rwanda, but it is included here because it does powerfully illustrate the most important change in the new Rwanda. Nowadays, Mary farms her small plot of land in Nyamata village in the Eastern Province, fifty kilometres from Kigali. Aged fifty three she lives with her three surviving children; the oldest is twenty one. She is a genocide survivor.

Seventeen years after the events, she vividly remembers the day the Genocide caught up with her family and she watched as her husband and four of her children were hacked with machetes, thrown into a pit and left for dead. In the chaos she managed to run with one child on her back. Her house was burned and the cattle stolen by her immediate neighbours with whom they had lived for years. She fled to the forest and travelled only at night when most of the Interahamwe were drunk and raping women and small girls.

Eight days later she learned that her husband and four other children were dead. She says that that was the time she lost the will to live. She no longer feared death; she thought it might come any minute. After four days and nights of horror she made it across the border into Burundi where she was reunited with her other two surviving children. Mary was traumatised and lost the desire to bathe or eat.

After the Genocide she was repatriated to Rwanda. She says 'I could not socialise with anyone, there was no more love left in me and I treated everyone like animals.' Then she was helped by the Christian Prison Fellowship of Rwanda's Director, Gashagaza Deo, who was preaching to the survivors. The survivors were taught the word of God and the need for forgiveness and reconciliation. Gradually, with God's help she was able to forgive those who had killed her family members.

One of her next door neighbours, Leonard Rucogoza, confessed to taking part in killing her family and was sent to jail, where he apologised and asked forgiveness. He said 'I am one of those who committed the Genocide. I was imprisoned in 1995 and Pastor Deo found me and others in jail and preached the Gospel to us. I wrote to my victims and apologised. On 5th January 2005 I was released by a Presidential pardon.' At first he had to go to a training camp to prepare for life back in his village.

He confesses that he was scared of reprisals when he returned, but no one attacked him. Gradually he was able to face his neighbours and resume normal life and, amazingly, lives next door to Mary Izajiriza again. Mary now says, 'He is the first person I go to when I have a problem.' This is the power of the Gospel of Christ bringing reconciliation to the new Rwanda.

Could ethnic violence return to Rwanda? It seems unthinkable that anyone would try to stir up the same atmosphere of hatred that preceded the Genocide of 1994. In 2003 the new constitution was approved by a referendum. It allows for Presidential elections every seven years, with a maximum of two terms. Paul Kagame was elected in 2003 and re-elected in 2010 with 93% of the votes cast. Opposition, inside and outside the country condemned the election as unfair because some leading opposition candidates were intimidated or banned from standing. Amnesty International expressed its concern at some of the reports. However, observers from the African Union and the EU reported that the elections were free and fair. The candidate who came from her home in Holland set out her agenda based on ethnicity, which will not be tolerated in the new Rwanda.

There is no doubt that Paul Kagame, with his military background, is a tough operator. He allows no one to try to resurrect the old ethnic divisions. There are politicians and activists associated with the former government and the Interahamwe who want to gain power by appealing to the Hutu ethnic majority for support, based on ethnic lines. Some even go as far as wanting to rewrite the recent history of Rwanda and downplay the Genocide. 'Genocide denial' is a crime now in Rwanda.

Most international observers applaud Kagame for the way he is seriously attempting to change the traditional ethnic divides and unite Rwanda. The international community has responded to his efforts with aid and approval. In 2017 Kagame is due to stand down and not seek election again. This will be the test that can separate him from many other African presidents who have stayed in office by repression and fraud for decades.

Any international commentators that take out their ideological magnifying glasses to point out imperfections in Rwanda's journey to 'western style democracy' need to bear in mind that it is often pointed out, that it took the West a thousand years to reach their own varieties of democracy and some now expect ancient African societies to make this jump overnight. The amazing progress that Rwanda has made should be encouraged and applauded. In 2009 Rwanda was admitted to the Commonwealth and English replaced French as the language of education.

See Apendix 1 on page 205:'The God of Miracles' The testimony of Jean (John) and Viviane Gakwandi during the 1994 Rwanda Genocide.

CHAPTER NINETEEN

Retyrement not retirement

With his 'official' retirement approaching, Ken had to think about his replacement. He was aware that his recommendation would carry a lot of weight with the House of Bishops. It was important that the new incumbent should have no 'baggage' or 'skeletons in the cupboard' from the Genocide. In preparation for the new Bishop, Ken had organised the building of a house for his successor. He had his eye on a Ugandan clergyman working as an evangelist with the African Evangelistic Enterprise, Geoffrey Rwubusisi. He spoke the right language because he came from an area of Uganda where the Rwandan language is spoken. His wife Mary was a refugee from Rwanda. He saw the qualities in him that would be needed for the role.

The diocesan synod elected him unanimously. The House of Bishops was happy with the choice and unanimously endorsed him. He travelled to Cyangugu and took two teaching seminars before finally moving in. Ken timed his departure so that they overlapped for two months to enable Ken to show Geoffrey the work and share thoughts and vision. During Ken's last month he worked on setting up computers and the internet in the offices and in the guesthouse. He even brought a road roller out from England and worked hard on the access roads to all the new buildings, rolling in stones and gravel to prevent slipping in the rainy season!

On 25th February 2001, Geoffrey Rwubusisi was consecrated as the new Bishop of Cyangugu by the

Archbishop of Rwanda alongside the Archbishop of Uganda, who was the preacher, and nineteen Bishops from Rwanda, Burundi, Uganda, Tanzania and Congo. Ken handed over his 'throne' and Episcopal staff. The President of Rwanda was expected at the ceremony and great preparations were made accordingly. However, on the great day a message came from the Prime Minister's office that His Excellency was still at a conference in Tanzania so he was sending the Prime Minister in his place. The Consecration service went smoothly and was only drummed out by heavy rain for a short time.

When the service ended the Prime Minister made a speech. He wished the new bishop well and his speech showed that he had a good grasp of the local situation. He then said the Rwandan President had sent him, accompanied by nine Cabinet ministers, to thank Ken for the development work in Cyangugu. He called him over and handed him a large parcel which contained two framed pictures. One was a text in Kinyarwanda which said, 'Let us trust the Lord'. The other was a scene of cattle on the hills of Rwanda, beautifully embroidered and framed. Ken felt greatly honoured to have these gifts from the President of the country. He later had a letter from the President saying he was sorry he was unable to get to the service, but promised to visit the projects he hadn't yet seen. He has since frequently spent days at the Peace Guest House where he held a conference with a thousand delegates in the conference hall.

The new Bishop appointed Ken to the honorary post of 'Bishop Emeritus' of Cyangugu. He returned to England and retired from his two parishes of Ashburnham and Penhurst and had the great pleasure of receiving his first pension cheque from the Church of England Pension Board.

Before Ken left Rwanda he was called by the British Ambassador, Mr Graeme Loten, who told him that he was to be awarded the **OBE** (Officer of the Order of the British Empire) in recognition of his work in East Africa. When he returned home, he received a letter from the Palace confirming the award which would appear in the New Year's Honours list.

On 27th March 2001, Jill and Ken together with their daughter Jane and their son Michael drove to Buckingham Palace. As they drove down the Mall they saw that the Royal Standard was flying above the Palace, indicating that Her Majesty the Queen was in residence. Their car was searched both inside and underneath then they were ushered through the gates to a parking area. Dressed in his Episcopal shirt and collar and the hired top hat and tails and with the family also looking very smart, they walked into the Palace and were ushered to their respective places.

At Buckinham Palace with Jane and Michael

In the very brief moment with Her Majesty Ken was able to tell the Queen a few facts about Rwanda. Ken later sent her a short video and some pictures, which she was kind enough to comment on. Ken never in his life imagined that he would ever be speaking to the Queen about Rwanda, but there he was at the Palace where once his father loved to go to see the changing of the guards and hear the bands play as they marched their way through this long-established and much loved ceremony.

Lawrence Barham may have spent forty years as a missionary in Africa, but he always loved Buckingham Palace, the Guards and the bands. He used to tell his children how you can distinguish the different regiments of the Guards by the arrangement of the buttons on their red tunics. He was born in London and never lost his love for the great city. In Uganda he started companies of the Boys Brigade and obtained instruments for them from England. He had a band in Burundi that boasted a big drum, side drums, bugles and cymbals.

Ken thinks his father deserved this honour more that he did, but the life's work of many wonderful men and women inevitably go without recognition and sometimes even unseen. Ken could only imagine how very thrilled his father and mother would have been to see Ken, Jill and two of their grandchildren at the palace on this special day of recognition and honour, had they still been alive. However, there will come a time and a higher ceremony, when all the records of hard work, faithfulness and sacrifice will be revealed and full recognition given. On that day the recipients' fitting response will be to cast their crowns down before the throne of God.

In 2005 Ken received further recognition for his work in Rwanda, when he received a letter from the Archbishop of Canterbury informing him that he was to receive an honour at Lambeth Palace 'for services to the Anglican Communion'. Ken and Jill attended together with their daughters Jane, Sue and her son Joshua and one of their nieces Tanya, and parked at the Palace by the River Thames. There were twelve people receiving 'The Cross of St Augustine' in a moving service, with a choir from St Paul's Cathedral. They were given a conducted tour of the Palace and had tea with the Archbishop.

The Lawrence Barham Memorial Trust (LBMT) which had been registered by Ken back in 1985 has been the main vehicle for channelling funds that he and Jill had raised for developing the diocese of Cyangugu. By the time of the Trust's silver jubilee, over £3,000,000 had been raised through the charity. This is a remarkable amount in any country, but in Africa, where the pound and the dollar still go a long way, all the more valuable. However, the charity's remit and scope were wider than this one diocese. Inbuilt into the name of the charity is the word 'Memorial'. It was Ken's intention that the charity would be able to build on the work done by his father and mother, Lawrence and Julia, over the many years that they ministered in East Africa.

At Lambeth Palace

Once Ken had officially retired, he was free from the responsibility of running a parish in England and developing a new diocese in Cyangugu. Ken decided not to visit Cyangugu for the first two years after his retirement. He wanted the new Bishop, Geoffrey Rwubusisi, to feel free to develop his own ministry without having Ken visiting twice a year. Ken felt that if he continued his visits, the people would tend to still look to him for leadership and he didn't want to undermine the new leader.

This enabled Ken and Jill to concentrate on raising funds to help the wider Church in East Africa. In Uganda they helped with the development of the Bishop Barham University College, a constituent college of the Uganda Christian University. The original building which Ken's parents had built was still there in the heart of the campus and houses the chapel. They helped to build the Principal's house, purchased a large server for the hundred computers in the university library, and helped pay for the purchase of five former missionary houses for the teaching staff. Funds were also raised to build the ground floor of a four storey women's hostel. In Burundi they helped restore the diocesan cathedral, built by Ken's father in 1940 and also the college he built, now called the Bishop Barham Theological College.

Cyangugu was not forgotten. Funds were raised to improve the very popular 'rondavels' at Peace Guest House by having ceramic tiles laid on the floor of all five. Their son Michael had started the building of the rondavels some years earlier. He travelled out with two volunteers, Paul-Andre Wilton and Joel Jardine. They invited one Rwandan young person from each parish to work with them, building with locally burnt clay bricks and locally made cement. They completed the first one and local builders followed with the next four. They were thatched by a team of Ugandans, bringing special grass from Sesse Island in Lake Victoria.

Rondavel 5 at Peace Guest House, by Lake Kivu

Ken engaged a Rwandan builder, John Mugabutsinze to supervise the building and employ hundreds of local people at a good rate of pay. To fund the ongoing expenses, Ken has also completed the construction of four first class, modern houses for rent, to generate income for the diocese. He completed one each year for four years. These are considered as good quality housing and are now rented by lawyers and other important people in the town. Additional classrooms have also been added to the schools. Every new building project was fully paid for and no debts were incurred.

In 2006, the Diocesan Bishop in Butare, the university town of Rwanda, had been targeted by a number of people who made false accusations against him. Some of them were serious and it had reached the national press. The synod met and decided to give the bishop twelve months sabbatical leave while the accusations were dealt with. In 2007, the Archbishop of Rwanda asked Ken if he would go and spend as much time as he could at the diocesan headquarters to help with the leadership of the diocese. Ken was trusted by the Archbishop and the other clergy, as a person able to bring Godly judgement into the situation.

Ken still has a small house there, which, as a memorial to his mother, he had built in 1984 with money given instead of flowers at her funeral. Remarkably, this was the only house untouched in Butare in 1994 when so many were looted. Over the next two years, Ken spent most of his time in that role, making sure that he travelled back home regularly to Jill. If she had thought that Ken's official retirement meant that she would now see more of her husband, it was not to be; at least not for a while. Jill patiently dealt with the absence of Ken and continued to be active in the church and fund-raising activities. She sometimes travelled with him on his trips, but they always needed to find her air fares from their modest pensions, and any spare money they had was inevitably consumed somewhere in the ministry.

Although Ken had been brought in to steady the diocesan ship in Butare, the role gave him further opportunity to bring his own vision to bear in the situation. So it was inevitable that Ken, once again, began to build!

Shalom House, Butare

He built an income generating guest house, which he called 'Shalom House'. This was a two storey house with eight large bedrooms, all en-suite with hot showers, satellite TV, double or single beds and large mosquito nets. Both floors, the lounge, dining room and the kitchen all have ceramic floor tiles, which he had found were so popular in Cyangugu. In 2008 The Bishop of Butare resigned in order to complete his PhD in Strasbourg University. When a new Bishop of the Diocese was consecrated in 2008, Shalom House was used by all the Bishops who came for this special occasion.

The house then continued to receive guests and generate income for the diocese.

*   *   *

At the time of writing this biography, Ken is a relatively healthy and fit septuagenarian and the ministry in Rwanda continues. Their friends and family were not surprised that for Ken and Jill, being 'retired' has a very different meaning to that which is understood by most people! No doubt their work will last as long as their health permits and God leads them.

Ken and Jill's ministry both in Africa and at home is a very unusual story. God in His wisdom decided that they needed to be based in an English parish, to enable them to – quite literally – build on the revival ministry of Ken's parents, in the part of Africa to which they had committed their working lives. God engineered their circumstances to guide them in a direction that, at first, they couldn't understand, but accepted.

From Ken's early days at boarding school, God developed in him a personality that thrived on hard work, enthusiasm and multi-tasking. The schoolboy, who, after an early setback, became a good Christian witness, dramatically improved his academic work, excelled at a variety of sports, and developed the enthusiasm and energy that would be the hallmark of his life's ministry. His leadership gifts were also developed as he was given responsibilities by the school. He was what is sometimes called an 'all-rounder'.

Ken's early years in Africa, the wonderful heritage of his parents, the traits he developed at school, all were planned by God and combined to build in him the qualities that he would need for the remarkable ministry to which God would later call him. He responded enthusiastically and with remarkable energy to that call; God gave him Jill who supported and shared the vision, and God's kingdom in East Africa has benefited from their obedience. They are the first ones to say, *'To God be the glory'.*

Ministries in Kigali

RWANDA *'Rising from the ashes'*, is definitely worth a visit to see the amazing recovery of a devastated country due to good leadership and the prayers of many people around the world. Visitors can safely travel to any part of the country.

The God of Miracles –

The testimony of Jean (John) and Viviane Gakwandi during the 1994 Rwanda Genocide.

The Genocide of 1994.

When the genocide broke out publicly on the evening of April 6th, 1994, we – our family – received a promise from the Lord without knowing exactly what was happening. However, we felt that God was speaking to us. We received a Word through that evening's Daily Light reading – Proverbs 18:10 and Deuteronomy 33:26-27 [1]. The following morning, April 7th, at about 6.00am, killers arrived at our compound. By that time quite a large number of people we knew were already dead, including our next door neighbour. Ready to storm our compound, killers rang the gate of the compound bell, but the Lord told us not to open up. Instead all seven of us were led to go and hide in the storeroom of our kitchen, about two by two meters in size. We were praying and asking God to blind and confuse our attackers – which He eventually did. They shot the gate open and as they approached the house shot at the windows and doors shattering all the glass. Failing to find us they left

---

[1]   Proverbs 18:10 – The Name of the Lord is a strong tower; the righteous run into it and are safe.

Deuteronomy 33:26-27 – There is no one like the God of Jeshurun, who rides on the heavens to help you and on the clouds in his majesty.

The eternal God is your refuge, and underneath are the everlasting arms. He will drive out your enemy before you, saying, 'Destroy him!'

after some 15-20 minutes – I do not quite remember! My only question was: 'Why?' What had we done? Weren't they mistaken?' I just couldn't understand why we were being hunted like criminals.

We had to stay in the storeroom for 37 hours. We made no sound and avoided any movement because we believed killers were still around. We had no desire to eat or drink anything. Jessie our little daughter, who was four years old at the time, lay on the floor under a shelf because there was not enough space anywhere else. Despite having a stubborn cough at that time, she miraculously managed to discipline it and coughed without making a sound!

During the night, I had managed to pull a telephone line into our hiding place. We were thus able to communicate with some friends (whispering of course) who told us what was going on outside. We learnt that many people had been killed including the Prime Minister Agatha, some Government Ministers, and some of our friends. These included Thomas Kabeja and his entire family. Our friend and brother in the Lord, Israel Havugimana (and his children), spoke with us until around 11.30 am that day. He told us that Presidential Guards had come and stolen his money. Viviane warned him that they would come back. They did and he was killed with his family that same afternoon. (April 7th)

The telephone helped us to link up with our partners in Holland and through them other friends world-wide. We know that through them, the message of our distress reached around the world and many Christians started to pray for us.

Friday, April 9th – 9.30am.

During the night, God had revealed to me that something was about to happen at 9.30 am and at 9.15 am I asked everybody to pray. And indeed, killers came back for the second time at 9.30. We again asked the Lord to blind them and confuse them.

This time the search seemed to take much longer. They tried the doors and shot again through windows. They even shot the wardrobe, thinking people were hiding in it, and the beds, in case people were hiding underneath. They eventually climbed up to the little window of our hiding place. We thought it was the end of our lives, since they often used to throw hand grenades into rooms through a window. Indeed they said they would throw one, but they were retained from doing it. I saw Viviane preparing our children to die, committing their souls to the Lord. The children said yes with a nod of the head. Within me, I said 'NO'. I wanted to believe what the Lord had told us and knew to be true. I kept on praying in my heart asking God to confuse the killers. They finally left. This confirmed what Viviane had experienced during the night. She had seen a vision of an army of angels surrounding our house. I believe we were under strong divine protection.

Nevertheless, we decided that it was time to leave that particular hiding place. The problem was how and where to go! God had planned it His way. For a few months, I had been learning German. An idea struck me to call Marianne, our German language teacher who had always come over as very compassionate and concerned. She hastened to do all she could to save us. We do not know just how many doors she knocked at, seeking someone to be our rescuers and help on our behalf. Finally she succeeded. We had managed to set up a system of telephone call codes and signs so that any killers could not get through to us and so be able to find out that we were still alive and where we were hiding. In fact the second attack had occurred because someone who called us realized that we were still alive, and then sent killers to finish us off. So we decided not to respond to any further phone calls. In spite of all this, Marianne eventually convinced the Swiss Ambassador herself to come to our house, where we were hiding.

Marie-France, the Swiss Ambassador, is a very brave woman. Driving along the streets of Kigali, she saw people killing and being killed. She was not afraid to go and save scores of people, many of whom are alive today and can testify to that effect. May God bless her abundantly.

Viviane had told Marianne that our main gate was open because bullets had damaged it the previous day. Viviane would put a red cloth in the front yard as a sign to Marie-France that that was our house and hiding place. A miracle happened. As Marie-France arrived, there were no killers prowling about. Our street was empty. The killers she saw on the next street were short of petrol and they couldn't follow her to see where she was going and for what reason. The Swiss Flag on the right side of Marie France's car was really an added tool ensuring safe passage. Surely, for me, the white cross on the red background symbolizes rescue, Jesus giving Himself for us! I love this flag with its cross and all that means to me! We all managed to squeeze into her small 5 seater Toyota saloon, making 8 of us altogether. Before leaving and within the space of a few minutes, most of us managed to put on 2 pairs of trousers, 2 shirts and 2 jackets. Some clothes were riddled with bullet holes. In such haste, I realized later that the little money we had at home was in a jacket I had put on not realizing that it had holes in the pockets. However, in such circumstances this was not important. As we left our home No 29 Avenue Kamuzinzi, we noticed a few metres ahead, on the left side, a roadblock manned by Presidential Guards. Whether we managed to pass unnoticed, or whether they were not interested in checking who we were, I will never know. What I do know, is that that God had given us the promise (Pr 18:10 and now in addition the whole of Ps 91[2]) and that we had prayed asking God to blind the killers.

In the twinkling of an eye, we had arrived safely at Marianne and Wolfgang Schmeling's residence in rue Akagera. There, we met two other refugees.

Wolfgang worked for 'Swiss Cooperation'. Like their neighbour, Marie-France, this couple is a very loving family. We realize that it was dangerous for them to take the risk of protecting people like us. Even Belgian soldiers were being killed because they protected the unwanted Prime Minister. It is not easy to understand how people could risk their own lives to protect us. We owe them a lot.

Wolfgang and Marianne are really wonderful people. Their house has only 3 bedrooms. We were nine refugees in their house plus their family of four. Had they had the opportunity to welcome more refugees in their house, they would have done it with great joy. In fact, on Saturday April 9th, Marie-France managed to rescue another distressed family from the suburb of Nyamirambo made up of eight people and they came to join us. We now numbered twenty-one in all. Marianne and Wolfgang shared everything they had with us, and they totally identified themselves with us. The Schmelings are a family of three and lived with their guard, Alphonse and a dog, Lola. So, this small family of three or four had to share their provisions with seventeen more people. I believe this was love in action. We also learnt that Marie-France had thirty-five people in her house nearby.

This was unique because at that critical time, nobody seemed to be interested in what was happening and very few people were concerned about the fate of those who were targeted. I believe that if all those who could have helped, and had the capacity to act, had done so, then very many more lives would have been saved.

17 rue Akagera was to be our home for eighty-nine days. There, we had to be very quiet for all but a few hours every day. Threats from the street were never far away. We were advised not to go out. Just a few minutes after our arrival, we heard cries in the street and had to go and hide in the toilets. It was essential that everyone believed that only the Schmelings were there.

Then, all foreigners were warned to leave the country immediately. It was hard for Wolfgang and Marianne to leave us. But they were under pressure from all sides to leave. We too understood that this was necessary. So, two days later they left. Another three of us were given the opportunity to leave with them. All who left reached Switzerland a few days later, after a short stay in Bujumbura, Burundi.

Meanwhile outside, suspicions remained that there were still some people in our house. We learnt this from the watchman, Alphonse, who was a very good man, a born again Christian. Because of his ethnic group, he was not under threat. Trying to be of help he told us to hide, keep very quiet and be sure not to do anything to rouse suspicion that people were still in the house. So, we drew all the curtains, and some of us hid in wardrobes – fortunately there were many in that house. Another hid in a chimney. This left some with only the beds to hide under. No one was allowed to smoke – even if they were addicted to it.

We remained in darkness for almost a whole week. During that time, God cared for us in a very particular way.

My experience is that wherever you may go with Him, His grace is always with you and enables you.

For instance, at that time of great agony and stress, we realized that human beings need lots of fluid. Incredibly our needs were supplied because it rained very hard, making a lot of noise on our roof made of iron sheets. This meant that we could crawl out from our wardrobe and get some water from the bathroom. Otherwise the noise we made moving around would have drawn attention to us and it would be all over.

We could only communicate by whispering when we were sure that no one was around. In the darkness, behind curtains during the day, or at night, our vision was limited. We couldn't speak because killers were always patrolling around the house threatening the guard that he would be killed if people were found inside the house.

Sometimes we heard them boasting about their record of killings, some saying that they had killed up to twenty people or more single handed. Down the street, just ten metres from the house, we knew that day after day people were being killed at the roadblock nearby. Some we knew well.

Back on Saturday, April 10th, as I was wondering how we could survive without food, God gave us this word in Proverbs 10:3 – 'He will never let the righteous go hungry'. God never failed to fulfill this promise to us. The threat became a reality on the second day of our imprisonment in the wardrobes. Little Jessie was with me in my cell, (measuring 50cms by 50cms wide and 120cms high). As time progressed I could count her ribs as I held her. She was getting thinner and thinner. I was afraid she was about to die of hunger.

Then something fell on my knee in the dark. I took it and felt that it was somehow soft. I smelt and it smelt like chocolate. When I tasted it, it really was chocolate falling from the upper shelf of my cell! I stretched my arm up and found that the shelf was full of chocolates and all kind of sweets. It was like unexpected manna received from above coming at just the right time. After our release, we learnt that Tabitha, the Schmelings' four-year-old daughter, had regularly been sent treats from her grandma. These were stored away and given to her now and again. So much was left over because her mother wanted to protect her teeth!

In our confined 'prison cells', things like this happened, which showed us the tremendous care of the Lord. David says in Psalm 23: "Even though I walk through the valley of the shadow of death, I will fear no evil, for you are with me".

I suffer from sciatica in my right leg. With this condition it is almost impossible to remain bent up, crouching for days on end. Yet I did! As for Viviane, she was prone to attacks of asthma every time she opened a cupboard. Yet now, she had to live in one! But amazingly she didn't sneeze even once! We now know who is God and who satan is!

Discovery

On Friday 15th, after only five days in our cells the killers discovered us! With us in hiding was a priest who had managed to contact an army chaplain on the phone. The chaplain came to pick him up. As he left it was noticed that there were other people inside. We were all ordered out. I was the first. The Presidential Guard were accompanied by a mob with grenades, guns, and with spears, bows and arrows. One of them asked permission to throw a grenade at us. I felt no fear.

Quite by chance, the soldier in charge happened to be one of my patients. He asked me what I was doing there. I said we were in hiding and that if he needed to know he could inspect my house and see the bullet holes, where we had been shot at, all around. He asked me how many other people were with me, and who they were. I said they were all members of my family – although I didn't even know their names because we lived in darkness. Then the thugs lowered their weapons and told us to go back into the house. We were ordered to stay there. Our case would be handled later.

We were somewhat relieved, although we knew for certain that from now on our days were numbered. But it meant that we were now able to draw back the curtains and let in the light. We could sit in the living room and could openly use Marianne's stores and eat some food. We could even talk a little. We had nothing more to hide. We were discovered. The Officer came and collected our telltale identity cards. The identity cards marked our ethnic group. It was these cards that condemned hundreds of thousands to die. However, in my own heart I still believed that we were going to survive.

Later that same evening the Presidential Guard Officer came back accompanied by two other soldiers. One of our number, Claude, was taken to the nearby road block and killed there. He had been the first refugee to come to the Schmelings'.

That night the guards told our house girl that our very hours were numbered! Our reaction was to pray. We prayed for these killers. We asked God to make them forget that we were there, alive: and the Lord started to soften their hearts.

Days passed, in which the front line of the battle between the troops of the advancing Rwanda Patriotic Army (the RPA) reached the area of the town where we were hiding. As they approached bombs began falling everywhere including our garden in the residential quarter. We rejoiced at this. The battle was so fierce that our killers were afraid to walk about. But bullets were flying everywhere both in the compound and the house.

Once I escaped a bullet, the size of a finger, which penetrated both the window and a door hitting the floor, at the very moment I was walking there. A bomb (one among many) exploded in the front garden of the house and shrapnel broke the doors and windows but amazingly not one of us was harmed. When some of us thought it safer to be outside in these circumstances, the Lord told us to stay indoors (Isaiah 26:20) [3].

Our God has a wonderful sense of humour. There was a tree in the garden laden with ripe avocados. For obvious reasons, we couldn't risk going out to pick them. Bullets were continually flying around. Then, a bomb fell and hit the tree. All the avocados fell to the ground. The Lord knew we needed them! Not only that, but for several days, mushrooms sprung up from nowhere around the house, even through cracks in the cement floor. I do not remember how many days we fed on them, but they were very delicious. Like manna, we had to pick them everyday, because they spoilt if we tried keeping them overnight. Our guard said he had never seen this before in the compound.

We were supplied with water in different ways, all miraculous. The mains water system failed on several days. When the water tank emptied, water came from nowhere to fill it and then it emptied again. Once when it emptied, it unexpectedly rained in the middle of the dry season. God did this for us because we weren't able go out to fetch water like others normally do from the valleys. Miracles!

All this time more killings went on in the city and in our neighborhood. Once we learnt of people being massacred in the street just a few yards from the house. A young boy was shot and left bleeding on the side of the road for three days, begging to be finished off. Even this request was denied him and he was left to die. Three other young men were thrown

---

[3]   'Go, my people, enter your rooms and shut the doors behind you; hide yourselves for a little while until his wrath has passed by.'

into the latrines of a nearby guesthouse and stoned until they died. People who took refuge in church compounds around Kigali were killed on a daily basis in large numbers.

I learnt that my own mother was macheted and left bleeding for several days in a trench before she died. But this I did not hear until after the war. My grandmother, almost 99, was burnt alive, and my brother David, with his wife and five children, were thrown into latrines and buried alive. My father was in a way, fortunate. He was killed with a sword and his murderer said that he didn't make a sound. On my father's side alone I lost ninety-nine relatives who I can remember by name.

My father had had ten children of whom, apart from me, only two sisters remain (This was because they were married to men of the "good ethnic group"). All the others were wiped out together with their families, except that one of my brothers left behind his two children and a widow.

Delivery

Terrible atrocities were committed in the way that many were killed. Those who could pay large sums of money were accorded the 'privilege' of being shot or blasted by a grenade – a privilege that could not be given to many.

These terrible events continued until July 4th, when the Rwanda Patriot Army took control of Kigali. We couldn't believe our eyes or ears! We could now go freely outside into the sunshine: we could speak as loudly as we wished, or even sing! We hadn't been able to do this for three months.

We were horrified to learn of all the people that we knew who were no longer alive. We felt alone, very lonely. It was almost impossible to think about the future. We didn't care about our poverty, and material things meant nothing to us. All we needed was peace and freedom – nothing else.

And for this we were full of gratitude – gratitude to God, who alone brought about our survival. How, we asked ourselves, were we now able to walk about freely and be seen? – when only twenty-four hours before, these most basic of freedoms had been completely denied us. O Lord our God, You really are the God of the impossible!

Coming to terms with survival.

Psychologically, we were of course in a terrible state. However, the Lord was constantly by our side encouraging us. He spoke to us through his Word and we prayed almost unceasingly. We had three prayer meetings a day, and in the late evening we prayed a lamentation.

We were continually fed on God's word, and were comforted. However, it was more than uncomfortable to fully realize that we had survived when so many around us and in our neighbourhood, even next door, had been killed. All of us had been hunted down. Some we had heard being killed. Only we survived. Why?

Most of the time, we remained totally discouraged and full of fear. It was a very hard task for me to raise the morale of our group. I had to be strong enough to pull them up, when I too felt completely down! However, knowing that people around the world were praying for us renewed my strength. One of our regular prayers was to ask God to tell our brethren around the world that we were still alive and to enable them to keep on praying for us. It was so hard to believe that anyone could have survived in our part of the town. It further distressed us that we were so cut off from the rest of the world. There was no longer any telephone and no one to inform about what was happening. The only broadcast news we could receive on the Schmeling's FM clock radio was from the satanic RTLM network. This had actually been re-activated when a bomb had exploded in the garden. We hadn't known that there was one in the house before that. However, listening to RTLM was unbearable. To be honest, it was the voice of satan and I could never listen to it.

We felt isolated from the world outside. Fear, agony and despair were our daily bread. We became hardened, and we lost all natural emotions. No one could smile or laugh: be happy or sad: nor even weep or cry. We were all numb. One of the girls with us learnt that her fiancé had been killed. She showed no special reaction. Another one learnt that her parents in Kibungo had been beheaded and she didn't react at all. (We had heard about both these happenings at a time when the telephones were still working). When I learnt that my brother who lived in Kigali had been killed I assumed that my parents and all my other brothers and sisters had died as well, which eventually turned out to be true. But I too felt no emotion except feeling that my throat was dry. This numbness persisted for almost a year. Indeed, in reality we will never be as we were before this tragedy.

Another marked effect on what we went through is that children quite suddenly became little adults. They started both to reason and react like adults to various situations.

The reality of my own situation from a human and emotional point of view struck home to me in a meeting of about four hundred widows. They were all weeping and I wept too. Some of them have been literally left all alone, whereas before they had large families with many children. Others were very young women – between nineteen and thirty years old – newly married with one child, or as yet or none at all. Now they are stripped of every thing they owned. Their houses have been destroyed, they are physically mutilated – either losing one or more limbs, or one or both eyes for example. Many are disfigured. Others, not merely a few, were inhumanly raped. The list goes on.

They – all of them – have suffered immensely. The stories many tell are completely unbelievable. Some buried alive to die were later found still living in their graves. Some have crawled out from the middle of a pile of thousands of dead bodies. Some have huge scars from wounds that have healed over without any surgical aid. Indeed some of their stories are unbelievable from a scientific point of view. Miracles! And because of this they praise God and organise meetings in order to testify and praise His Name.

Indeed, so many of us have experienced the mercy of God and His faithfulness in a tremendous way. It is true that when you really have faith in Him you can never be disappointed. Another truth is that in times of terrible crisis, Christians, as someone has said, are at their best. Our Lord is a Living God. He hears our prayers and answers them. It is incredible to learn that when we asked God to urge people to pray for us, they did so. And, as they now thank and praise God because we survived, we in turn can thank Him because the reason for our survival is so that He might be praised.

God kept all the promises He gave to us when the genocide started. He protected our bodies, our souls and our spirits. He taught us to put all things in their proper place. We believe that many of us survivors during our trials made important vows to God, which we now need to keep.

We experienced how God cared for us in many ways. I sometimes wonder why even now I don't go mad. In April 1995, there are images on TV showing the bodies of about 23,000 people which have been exhumed at Murambi in the Prefecture of Gikongoro. At this location more than 40,000 people were killed. Amongst the bodies are two of my own brothers, David, Emmanuel and Vianney, and my sister, Veneranda and quite a number of cousins. Amazingly it does not drive me insane. Is not this the grace of God?

Most of those killed, if not all have gone to be with the Lord. For indeed, during those days, nearly everybody put their life into the Hands of God. That is why I can say that, paradoxically, the evangelization of this country has not failed. Hundreds of thousands of saints are now with the Lord. Perhaps the church as an institution has failed. And unfortunately brethren around the World are being wrongly informed and misled about the tragedy that has occurred here. Some so-called Christians are not telling the truth. I believe that our Lord Jesus has suffered greatly because of what happened. However, He is alive and He speaks. I am convinced that if any brother or sister in the Lord needs to know the truth about what position he should take and what to pray for, the Holy Spirit who is much more concerned than we are will lead him or her into all truth.

Every day, I see the effects of this tragedy on many people. Some are deeply traumatized, but they all want to know Jesus better and that has become our mission. We survived for this purpose. On April 27th 1994 at the climax of the genocide by which time most of my wider family had been exterminated, God gave me a wonderful word from Psalm 118:17. "I shall not die, but live to proclaim the works of the Lord". Such works of the Lord are always Good News, the "Gospel". They are for everyone – especially the desperate and the lonely – to be a comfort to them.

I think this is one of the most important messages for our country. Comfort. The Lord says: 'Comfort, comfort my people.' (Isaiah 40:1). He says again, in Matthew 11:28: 'Come to me all who are weary and burdened, and I will give you rest'. This same clear mission and responsibility is repeated in 2 Corinthians 1: 3-4: 'We are comforted so that we also can comfort others'. It is now time to do just this. We are called to lead all the desperate, the lonely, and the hopeless to Jesus Christ our Hope, who will give them the necessary comfort they need. Chief amongst those in need are widows and orphans, especially those who were raped and contracted HIV/AIDS as a result. They need special comfort and special care.

One lady, a widow, said recently that we did not survive in order to enjoy life. Not at all, but to fulfill our mission as God has now entrusted it to us. I agree with her. The situation is not the easiest. The killers are still there, and we survivors are their prime targets. Why? That question is difficult to answer, as God Himself knows. What I myself know and believe deeply in my heart, is that we, the survivors, are longing for His Kingdom to come amongst us. It is far better than anything else on this earth. People remain attached to material things when they have not lost loved ones, or many of their possessions. It is different when you lose everyone and everything of value to you. Then, you long for the treasure you cannot lose, and the life that cannot be threatened. All this we find in Jesus. We know now that God provides. If He has been able to feed us for ninety and more days in our dungeon how much more is He certainly able do it anywhere, at anytime and in any situation.

We know ourselves to be in the 'end times', and we want to obey the word of scripture: 'Be faithful even to the point of death' (Revelation 2:10). To my ears this sounds better in my own language, Kinyarwanda: "Ujye ukiranuka, uzageze ku gupfa".

Jean Gakwandi.

Note – Jean and Viviane's testimony, originally written in English, has been rendered into idiomatic English by long term friends of Jean and his family, Pat and Jeff Newth. No attempt has been made to edit it for content in any way.

Canon Stephen Simcox

If I started a conversation with the sentence "There were two bishops and a lorry" you may think I was starting a joke or at least a funny story. But this short story is about faith, prayer and commitment.

The year was 2006, it was my first trip to Rwanda with Bishop Ken and I was still getting to know him. We were in Butare. The day started with a simple breakfast and prayer. At this point I had not got a clear understanding about what this simple morning prayer at the start of the day meant to Bishop Ken. As the day unfolded I would remember that prayer.

In the compound was a lorry, a tipper lorry, and as we walked towards it I realised that this lorry, which was very new to the Diocese of Butare, was to be our transport for the day. Bishop Venuste, who shared a warm smile and a Rwandan greeting, joined us and I looked about for the driver of the lorry. I tried to stay composed as I was informed gently that Bishop Ken was the driver, Bishop Venuste was the navigator and I would be there to help.

The plan was to drive to a certain location where we would meet a willing task force who would fill the lorry with very large stones, which would be taken to another location to be used as the foundations for a new project building. It all sounds very easy and although I was bouncing around a bit, sitting on the engine, I felt safe between two Diocesan Bishops who seemed to know what they were doing.

Once the lorry was loaded we headed off to the drop point. This for me was where the simple but faithful prayer we had shared earlier in the day started to come to mind. The lorry was now full of heavy stones, the road that we had travelled on to the pick up point was now wet from the rain and I realised, far too narrow for our lorry if any other vehicle was travelling in the other direction. I also realised that where the side of the road we were travelling on stopped, a very deep drop began. I watched as Bishop Ken drove a lorry that was now very heavy on a wet mud road that was far too narrow, that had a serious drop if we were to lose grip. Bishop Ken negotiated the potholes and tried to stay away from the deep drop and then... there it was! Another lorry was heading up the hill. I made a quick assessment and came up with the answer, we are in trouble!

On this and many other journeys that I have been on with Bishop Ken, his faith in a God who hears our simple but heart felt prayers, makes up this formula, that even when things look difficult and dangerous, a way opens for God to work His wonders and for us to be amazed. Bishop Ken's quote of faith and prayer, "It will be alright, we have prayed". What I now realise is, Bishop Ken also knows that our God hears our simple but faithful prayer and answers our call.

To this day I do not know how we passed that other lorry without ending up at the bottom of a valley with a great load of stones on top of us. But we did and the day continued. I must finish this short story by saying that when we arrived at the drop off point, none of us knew how to operate the lorry's tipping facility; which is the introduction to another faith, prayer and commitment tale.